Business Matters

A freelancer's guide to business success in any economy

Elizabeth Frick

Business Matters

A freelancer's guide to business success in any economy

Copyright © 2013 Elizabeth Frick

Credits

Copy edit:	CJ Walker
Cover design:	Jennifer Neale Davis

Excerpt from *GUERRILLA MARKETING: Secrets for Making Big Profits From Your Small Business*, 3/e by Jay Conrad Levinson. Copyright © 1998 by Jay Conrad Levinson. Used by permission of Houghton Mifflin Company. All rights reserved.

Disclaimer

Trademarks

XML Press
Laguna Hills, California
http://xmlpress.net

First Edition
ISBN: 978-1-937434-22-9 (print)
ISBN: 978-1-937434-23-6 (ebook)

Table of Contents

Preface

I never finished the MBA that I started in 1980. That's actually good news.

When I launched my freelance business in 1990, not having completed (or remembered) any of my formal business school training meant that I would make more than a few mistakes as I lurched through good times and bad. But not applying MBA models to my business meant that I planned and grew my company, The Text Doctor, LLC,[1] organically; my business model fit me rather than forcing me into a business-school mode.

In the process, I learned that it was not enough to be technically smart and always passionate about my chosen disciplines of training and editing. I discovered that I had to become proficient in business planning, strategy, marketing, finance, and operations so that my business would succeed in any economy. This is probably true for most freelancers who migrate from corporate employment to self-employment. As employees, few of us became involved in strategic thinking and planning for our companies. That was management's job. Well, as freelance independents, we discover that suddenly we "are management," usually without any formal training in the tasks involved and often with little or no support.

As I gradually learned my (sometimes) painful lessons, I shared them in my column "Business Matters" in *Intercom*, the magazine of the Society for Technical Communication (STC),[2] from 2003 to 2012. Business Matters republishes those articles, substantially revised and arranged thematically. In addition, I have added several new chapters.

My goal is to provide freelance independents who are passionate about their discipline with the minimum training they need to direct or redirect their freelance, consulting, or service companies wisely. As you will learn throughout this book, it is not enough to just be technically smart—you will also have to be business-savvy to succeed in any economy.

---

[1] http://www.textdoctor.com
[2] http://www.stc.org

I'm also writing for potential freelancers. Just last night at a party, I spent a half hour discussing self-employment with a woman I had just met. This happens often when people learn that I have been self-employed since 1990. I am happy to share my experience with them, and actually, that's why I started writing my column. As you read, please check the Resource List[3] frequently, as I will update it often to provide you with useful links.

Acknowledgments

I'd like to start by thanking Richard Hamilton of XML Press for his boundless patience; this is my first book and also my first experience with XML, and I know I had to be told what to do more than once.

I am grateful to Betsy Frick (the other Elizabeth Frick) for passing on to me the opportunity to take over her STC *Intercom*[4] column for independent freelancers in 2003. Without this act of generosity, these chapters would never have been born. I am also grateful to my STC editors, Cate Nielan, Maurice Martin, and Liz Pohland for their gentle editorial guidance.

You'll notice many "quotations from the trenches"—useful suggestions from fellow STC members who responded to my requests for their personal experiences. Their sage advice rounded out my experiences as a freelancer (their names appear here in alphabetical order). Many thanks to Rahel Bailie, Rhonda Bracey, Andrea C. Carrero, Tony Chung, Janet S. Clifford, Mary Jo David, Carol Elkins, Alice Jane Emanuel, Paula Foster, Betsy Frick, Linda Gallagher, Beryl Gray, Suzanne Guess, Stacey Hall, Mindy Hoffbauer, Steven Jon, Rich Maggiani, Donna Marino, Kathleen McIlraith, Holly Mullins, Katherine Noftz Nagel, Pat O'Donnell, Sarah O'Keefe, Ginny Redish, Laura Ricci, Monique Semp, Thea Teich, Tammy Van Boening, Angela Wiens, Liz Willis, and Lyn Worthen.

I would also like to thank Jill Konrath for her quote about value propositions and specific measurable results and Stackpole Books of Harrisburg, Pennsylvania for allowing me to quote so freely from Bradford Angier's *Looking for Gold: The Modern Prospectors Handbook*[2].

---

[3] http://www.textdoctor.com/bizresources
[4] http://stc.org/intercom/

Introduction

CHAPTER 1

Could You, Should You, Go Independent?

Wouldn't it be nice if there were a test that you could take that would identify whether you are suited to start an independent business and succeed? I don't believe there is such a test available, and I'm not sure that I would trust it anyway. Succeeding as an independent requires many intricate decisions driven by interactive personality traits—and only you can determine if you have those traits and if you really want to succeed as an independent. This chapter may help you start your dialogue with yourself about going independent.

Every freelancer has a different story about how they launched their own business. I stumbled into freelancing after two different layoffs as a project manager developing educational software in the recession that began in 1990. In the midst of that recession, I was not thrilled about finding another job and facing more of the same—the hassle of daily commuting, difficult bosses, office politics, and layoff risks. So, with a little severance pay in hand, I printed business cards and went solo.

Good news, bad news about freelancing

If I had interviewed experienced freelancers before my plunge, they would have told me that there is good news and bad news in both employment and freelancing. You probably know about the benefits of employment: Steady pay, camaraderie with fellow employees, benefits packages, a desk, a computer, and software. You probably know the bad news as well, whether it is a difficult work group, a maniacal boss with unrealistic expectations, work that you don't really like, or the nagging feeling that you don't have any job security.

It is all so appealing, the freelance life: flexibility of schedule, clients who respect you, a fair amount of autonomy and control over the work, better pay per hour, diversification to balance the risk, a home office with a window, and the CEO title after your name! What could possibly go wrong? (Think: paying 15.3% FICA, your own health insurance, and the costs of your own office, all in the face of potential extended time without paid work. And then, after a long dry spell, you get five projects to work on at once! And some of these you accept not because you want to, but because you must so that you can feed yourself, your family, and that lovely cat that graces your office.)

And yet, many of my fellow independents have chosen self-employment for much or most of their careers. Some want the flexibility to raise their families outside corporate time-frames; some chose freelancing because they may not fit into a specific job title or job description in most organizations. Still others prefer to work early or late hours that don't mesh with corporate work schedules. And there's always the introvert who can easily interface with one client at a time but does not thrive in a group.

Why I believe that I have survived as a freelancer since 1990

I think I fit into almost all of the categories in the prior paragraph. As a medical editor and corporate trainer who specializes in teaching technical writing, I found that most companies, even large ones, need me only as a vendor, not as an employee. I relished the flexibility to volunteer in my kids' classrooms or stay home with a sick child and start work at 4 am to make up my time. (I still cherish that flexibility as I volunteer in my grandchildren's classrooms and play with them on their days off from school.) And although I am extroverted in my own classroom, I am intensely introverted when I work. A therapist once told me, "You have a great need for autonomy"; perhaps that's why I thrive when given a task, specifications, and a few directions and can go off to sit in my sunlit office and bang out the work. (For more about introversion, read Susan Cain's *Quiet*[4].)

If you have the luxury of continuing in your job while you assess your own success traits for freelancing, perhaps the questionnaire later in this chapter will help you think deeply about your future as an independent. I haven't run these questions through any kind of rigorous testing (I wouldn't even know how to), and I haven't provided any kind of rating scale for you. Instead, I invite you to journal your answers and perhaps share what you find with your loved ones, a trusted colleague, a therapist, or a business counselor; please also send me e-mail at efrick@textdoctor.com to let me know how well the questions worked.

Or you might just leap, as I did, and experience the exhilaration and terror of surviving as an independent—kind of like riding the roller coaster without having to pay to enter the amusement park!

Questionnaire: Is the Independent Life for You?

Environmental assessment (do you fit into a corporate or organizational environment?):

1. Do you work best in patterns and time frames that don't fit into a normal work day?
2. Is the work that you love more of a discipline or passion for you than a job title or job description?
3. Is your chosen work in a field that often gets cut first in corporate downsizing (such as marketing or training)?
4. Do you shun the drama of office politics?

Self-awareness:

1. Do you see freelancing as a commitment, not just an experiment?
2. Did you or do you have a family member who was/is successfully self-employed?
3. Do you naturally think strategically? What are some examples of your strategic thinking that have ended successfully for you?
4. Are you comfortable promoting yourself constantly?
5. Do you have a financial cushion or a source of income that can help you during your start-up phase?
6. Are you emotionally able to withstand periods of financial uncertainty caused by lack of work?
7. Are you extroverted enough that you get bored working by yourself?
8. Are you primarily self-directed (do you prefer autonomy)?

9. Are you primarily an optimist, a positive thinker?

10. Are you able to diagnose your own mistakes and failures and learn from them?

Structuring your life as a freelancer:

1. Do you have family responsibilities that might require you to have the more flexible work schedule of an independent rather than an 8 o'clock to 5 o'clock day (plus commute)?

2. Are you willing to work some intense days of long hours as a trade off for the more flexible schedule identified in the question above?

3. Do you like to work alone? Do you prefer to work alone?

Questions that could help you decide about going solo:

1. Are you willing to interview people who are already freelancing in the line of work that you want to do, then sit down with a business advisor to create a business plan, and then—and this is absolutely essential—put this plan aside until you have complete clarity that going independent is the right path for you?

2. Are you willing to share your plan with your spouse, significant other, or any other individual for whom you are responsible or to whom you are responsible?

3. Are you willing to take a personality test such as Strengths Finder 2.0[2] or the Myers-Briggs Type Indicator®[3] and have a business counselor or therapist help you interpret the results?

After answering these questions, you might expect a rating scale—like "1 to 6 'yes' answers, you may be suited to freelance life." So sorry: I could not presume to define such a scale for you—you are the only person who is qualified to compute your readiness after you work through the questions.

That being said, if you had more "yes" answers than "no" answers—does that tell you anything? And if you had one emphatic, non-negotiable, drop-

---

[2] http://www.strengthsfinder.com/home.aspx
[3] https://www.mbticomplete.com/en/index.aspx

dead "NO" answer (even, "Hell, NO!"), that may tell you more about your suitability for freelance endeavors than any scale could.

And if you do all your due diligence and still decide to go independent, use all the business tips that follow to build a solid, profitable business that will feed your soul AND you and your family as well. And that cat.

CHAPTER 2

Independents' Success Depends on Business Skills

Most freelancers who migrate from corporate employment to self-employment may recognize that as employees, few of us became involved in strategic thinking and planning for our companies—that was management's job. Well, freelance independents find that we ARE management and we ARE the company, usually without any formal training in the tasks involved or the desire to focus on the business aspects of our practice. This first chapter addresses how you might start thinking about strategy and operations so that your business can thrive.

Let's assume that you have done your due diligence by answering the questions in the section titled "Questionnaire: Is the Independent Life for You?" and have decided to go independent ... now what?

Many freelancers start their companies in times of tight employment. Others lurk, waiting for the opportunity to escape "captive employment." Independence seems attractive: less bureaucracy, less focus on business, more focus on our craft.

However, we soon discover that solo practitioners function first as a business and second as practitioners. Our work may feed our souls and pay the bills—today. If we ignore business matters, our practices will languish and may even fail. It is not enough to be "technically" smart in our disciplines—we have to be savvy in business to succeed in any economy. For me, this realization came as a shock: As an English major, I had deliberately avoided business and math courses in college.

Ironically, independents are much closer to business issues than we were as employees because we often perform the functions of all departments all the time. We must be the marketing manager, tech support, bookkeeper, and janitor of our company, struggling to make our businesses function efficiently and productively so that we can spend more of our time doing what we love. This chapter will help you start to move toward thinking of yourself as a business so that you can stay in business.

The small-business failure rate is about 50% of startups, according to the US Census Bureau. Or think positively: About 50% of startups succeed, and the basis of their success is careful planning and good business practices.

One cliché about career strategy says, "Do what you love; the money will follow." In this chapter, let's amend that to:

- Do what you love.
- Plan and operate an efficient, effective business.
- Enjoy the money that follows.

Start thinking of yourself as a business

Corporations recognize three main functions in their business structure:

1. Strategy (direction of the business)
2. Operations (methodology and structure of day-to-day functions)
3. Execution (delivery of services)

Independents often spend so much time in execution (delivering service) that we may have to ignore any consistent effort in strategy and operations. It is tempting to strive to be doing billable work all the time and, in any non-working time, to improve our technical skills. However, strategy and operations, if handled thoughtfully, will allow you to efficiently produce your service and enhance your income.

In this chapter, we will discuss strategy and operations in general. We won't address the execution category because that will be different for each reader (and that's what you know best, anyway).

Later chapters will focus more on specific strategic and operational issues such as business plans, marketing plans, and financial plans.

Strategy (business direction)

As employees, few of us became involved in strategic thinking and planning in the companies we worked for. That was the job of management, and we were often "just" the workers. Well, now you ARE management. Here is the minimum you need to know to direct your own business wisely.

Corporations that hire you expect you to operate as a business, not as someone freelancing between jobs. To operate as a business, you'll need to acquire at least the following right away:

1. Appropriate licenses
2. Tax ID numbers
3. Sales tax numbers if applicable
4. Assumed name
5. Business checking account
6. Business credit card

Not sure about your state's requirements? See the Resource List.[1] Many states publish free information; for example, Minnesota provides *A Guide to Starting a Business in Minnesota*,[2] a 366-page PDF. Other states offer similar, free products and downloads of necessary forms on their websites.

You usually don't need an attorney to establish these simple business practices, but brief consultations with an attorney may help. Once you're established, you need only schedule renewals of licenses and registrations.

Define yourself with a Mission Statement

When I first launched my independent practice, I accepted every contract offered. I was just too scared to turn down business. When anyone asked me what I could do for them, I said, "What do you need to have done?" I probably appeared desperate and unfocused, and my clients' contract offers reflected their perception that they could get me to discount my services.

---

[1] http://www.textdoctor.com/bizresources/
[2] http://www.positivelyminnesota.com/Data_Publications/Publications/All_Other_DEED_Publications/Guide_to_Starting_a_Business_in_Minnesota.aspx

Because I had not defined my business niche yet, they perceived me as a commodity and bid accordingly.

I didn't see any growth in income until I defined my Mission Statement. Essentially, your Mission Statement declares your purpose: "What do I do? For whom? And why?" Your Mission Statement keeps you focused—and keeps you from trying to be all things to all customers.

A good Mission Statement helps you build the right business because it also tells you what work to reject. Clients have asked me to write copy for their website or to work with them on government proposals. These projects, while interesting, do not fit my core business, so I have referred my clients to other independents with whom I network.

A clear Mission Statement also helps you to market your specific talents. When you can define yourself succinctly as a "Web designer" or "grant writer" or "science writer" or "medical editor," you have a better chance of explaining your skills to potential clients.

Write a business plan and update it every year

A business plan outlines business goals, expected income and expenses, pricing strategies, marketing plans, and many other items. Business plans vary across industries and company size. There's no "one size fits all" in business plans, although there are many templates. And your business plan is never final. See Chapter 3, *Business Plans Build Good Businesses*, for more information about business plans.

Look for books and software products that can help you as you plan your business, or consider taking a class through your local community college or through SCORE,[3] a nonprofit association dedicated to providing entrepreneurs with free, confidential, face-to-face and e-mail business counseling. Business counseling and workshops are offered at 347 chapter offices across the country.

---

[3] http://www.score.org/

The SCORE website for your local chapter lists classes. A recent look at my local chapter showed several courses for new entrepreneurs—all for under $50 (some were free).

Write a marketing plan as part of your business plan

As I interact with other independents, I find that their concept of marketing is underdeveloped. Because they are so good at their craft, they think clients will find them. Not so, as I learned early in my freelance career! Every business needs to define its product or service lines, determine audiences for products, research those audiences' needs, create marketing tools, and then market itself. Marketing is like swimming: If you stop, you'll sink.

Define your marketing budget as a percentage of your gross income. You might be tempted to avoid spending marketing money unless you view those expenditures as a required expense in your budget. Money spent on marketing usually doesn't produce results immediately and so, instead of sending out a newsletter or developing a website, independents may feel more comfortable buying a computer or some software—something they can see and use every day. Spending marketing money wisely and regularly is a good business discipline to learn. Read Chapter 18, *Building a Marketing Plan*, to learn more.

Operations (running the business)

You will need to think through all the nuts and bolts of operating your business—decisions in finances, technology, and procedures. We'll look at operational decisions in Part IV, "Operations."

I call my attorney, accountant, and financial planner whenever I have an important business decision. I have paid management consultants to help me draft my Mission Statement. If I were to incorporate, I would have a board of directors direct me. Sure, I'd rather not write out checks to pay for these services, but I see the value of good business advice in helping me develop a sound strategy or avoid tax penalties.

Write a financial plan, even if you're not seeking financing

If you've been receiving your paycheck after all deductions are taken, getting lump sum payments from clients may tempt you into thinking you have more money to operate your business than you actually do. You'll need to see the financial "big picture" and the flow of your finances:

1. Learn to use spreadsheets to help with budgeting and finance.
2. Determine how much to set aside for self-employment taxes each month (consult your accountant first).
3. Define when to pay yourself and how much to leave in your business account.
4. Decide how much to set aside monthly for retirement.
5. Carry the right insurance to protect you and your equipment.

I am not naturally comfortable with budgets and spreadsheets (my excuse is that I am a "word" person, not a "numbers" person). My financial plan helps me stay on target and avoid scrambling at the end of the year to fund my retirement account.

Have a technology plan

What kind of technology and software will you own? What is the minimum you can own and maintain? What is your plan to update your technology? Without a plan, I became "gadget girl"—I bought way more software and hardware than I needed because I rationalized that it would make me more productive. It didn't; it only reduced my profit. Now, I have a plan to up-grade my hardware and software and to take classes to maximize my use of these tools. A written plan helps me avoid impulsive purchases.

After a few minor computer and data disasters, I have also created a tech-nology back-up plan; one detail is my low-tech storm protection: Unplug everything every time I leave the office in thunderstorm season. (You may choose to back up automatically to the Cloud; however, I'm old-fashioned and do not trust Cloud security for my own and my clients' documents.)

Document your procedures

It seemed silly to me that a solo practitioner should formalize office procedures. However, once I invested a few hours documenting my business
practices, I've realized much greater efficiency. Since I'm not accountable
to any government agency (yet), I just use checklists. For example, I have
weekly, monthly, and yearly close-out checklists installed on my electronic
calendar. Other written procedures help me document activities I don't do
often enough to memorize, such as backing up e-mail addresses.

Moving toward good business practices

You may not be able to implement all these efficient business practices
simultaneously unless you have the luxury of going months without earning
an income. Instead, you can phase in these practices, perhaps working on
them for four hours a week, or two days a month, until you have structures
in place that work for you. Others might concentrate on one phase of their
business per quarter: marketing in the first quarter, finances in the second.
It's important to schedule this time on your calendar and protect it as vital
to your survival, because it is!

And you won't have to do your business planning alone. Use one of the
excellent resources listed in the Resource List.[4] Just get started, or if you
already have some of these practices in place, improve upon them. "Slow"
is fine as long as you're making progress. No one else but you can improve
your business practices, which will then improve your economic stability
and income.

In later chapters, we will focus on specific strategic and operational issues
such as business plans, marketing plans, and financial plans, as well as
documentation and procedures. We will also talk about some of the emotional issues you might encounter as you grow your business.

---

[4] http://www.textdoctor.com/bizresources/

CHAPTER 3
Business Plans Build Good Businesses

Business owners can get mired in details, deadlines, and detours. Your business plan is the map you'll need to document where you've been and where you should go. You'll need to be passionate about your work, but passion without discipline leads to distraction, delay, and disaster. Write a plan, revise it regularly, and consult it every time you make a decision.

In Chapter 2, *Independents' Success Depends on Business Skills*, we reviewed business strategies that independents can use to be successful. One of the most necessary business strategies is to build a business plan—without it, your independent practice will flounder.

Like most independents launching a business, I was long on skill and short on business acumen when I went independent in 1990. I had passion for my craft but no idea how to make money with it. I plunged right into self-employment, an alien in the world of entrepreneurs, completely unaware of return on investment, market niches, and business strategy.

One experience helped me understand what I might need to do. When we had built our house in 1984, our architect developed a blueprint. Once we signed off on the blueprint, we had to stick to our plans, which saved us from a lot of impulsive, expensive mistakes. We were committed and excited about our house, but passion without discipline would have led to costly overruns.

And so it is in business. My excitement, without discipline, led me into swamps of unproductive work. Finally, I sought help from SCORE[1] and with their assistance built a plan that has helped me survive in any difficult economy. You can, too.

---

[1] http://www.score.org/

The benefits of a plan

According to Hector Barreto of the U.S. Small Business Administration (SBA), small-business owners have motivation and courage to try and build a business, but they do not always have a realistic plan or the resources to keep going long enough to be successful. It is clear to me: I would not still be in business if I had not developed a business plan early in the life of my business—it has kept me alive.

A business plan is a document that outlines your business goals, expected income and expenses, pricing strategies, marketing plans, and other decisions. Business plans vary across industries and company size. There's no one right way to build your business plan, although you may find helpful templates in the Resource List.[2] And your business plan is never final (after our house was "finished," there were inevitable modifications and remodeling projects).

Owners write business plans for several important reasons:

1. Internal management (develop strategy, provide direction)
2. Marketing analysis (determine marketing strategy, project sales)
3. Financial management (define cash plan, budgets, tax considerations)
4. Loan applications (seek funds from an institution or individual)
5. Investment (seek capital from others in return for ownership)

A business plan helps you in smaller ways, too. The exercise of writing yours will help you understand the businesses you serve. When your clients mention their business plans, you'll understand how you can support them.

Loans and investment opportunities might not be on your horizon at first, but writing your plan as if a banker would be looking at it will help you develop your numbers seriously and provide a yardstick for reality: What risks do you really face in starting or running your business? Are your projections realistic? If you show your plan to a trained advisor (for example, a SCORE counselor, usually a former executive), he or she can help you determine whether your assumptions are in line with the current economy.

---

[2] http://www.textdoctor.com/bizresources/

Another important benefit of a plan is that the language you write, particularly in the marketing sections, can form the basis of your website home page and other marketing materials.

Breaking down the plan

A business plan usually consists of a narrative and several financial spreadsheets. Both of these appear in sections such as Financial Forecast and Competitive Environment. Your narrative should include your Mission Statement and your objective. Write these before tackling the rest of the narrative. Your Mission Statement reduces your business plan to a one-paragraph driving force, the governing criteria for decision processes that must be made in day-to-day implementation.

Your objective includes the reason for your company's existence, your vision and expectations for the company, and your company's position within your competitive environment.

No formal standard exists for business plans, but you might consider any of the following common sections:

1. Executive summary
2. Company description
3. Products and services
4. Financial forecast
5. Business structure
6. Competitive environment
7. Competitive analysis
8. Competitive advantage
9. Marketing plan (including a market description, market definition, target customers, and market opportunities)
10. Business strategy
11. Keys to success (why you'll be successful).

Write the Executive Summary section last and include all the information that you would cover in a five-minute interview. An Executive Summary offers a clear, concise overview of the business and entices the reader to move on to the body of the plan. All points addressed in the body of the plan should be summarized in this section (which is why you write it last!).

Now the benefits of writing down your plan become obvious. If you carry your plan in your head, you'll keep revising it in your head. I revise my plan (on paper) around the first of each year when business is often slow. I first write down all the new opportunities that presented themselves over the past year to see if I can capitalize on them and still stay true to my Mission Statement. I brainstorm ideas for developing new products, new courses, and new market niches. I plan opportunities to learn new software and develop new ideas. All of this forms the basis for my updated business plan.

I keep my old plans in a notebook. It's really fun to look back five years later and see how much my business has grown. I celebrate new procedures that have made me more productive. I recognize continued weaknesses and fears and try to visualize how much more successful I would be if I could overcome them.

Why I believe in business plans

Don't let the concept of a business plan scare you, especially financial sections intended for potential lenders. If you are seeking financing, get someone to help you with the spreadsheet section. If you're not trying to borrow money or find investors, at least put the numbers down to the best of your ability as a useful discipline. Even I, an English major who scrupulously avoided math classes all through college, have learned to do sales forecasts and budgets in spreadsheets.

I sometimes cringe when new independents say they'll do any project a client wants because they need the money. That reminds me of my attitude when I was an employee—"You've bought me; now tell me what to do." As a fledgling independent, I may have had to take on every project, regardless of merit, but today, I can't afford that type of thinking. Instead, I weigh each project, marketing effort, and decision against my plan.

Be sure to check the Resource List[3] to see sample business plans and download templates that can get you started. Consider getting a mentor from SCORE; my mentor gently led me through the process and provided support and discipline in the beginning when I was really struggling.

Read on to learn about additional planning documents, including strategic plans and marketing plans.

---

[3] http://www.textdoctor.com/bizresources/

Business Strategy

CHAPTER 4
Attracting Perfect Customers: Developing Your Strategic Plan

Having a strategy is crucial to success in business. To drive business de-cisions, independents need a strategic plan as part of their business plan. While there are many books that can help you develop your strategic plan, the most useful book that I ever read on this topic is **Attracting Perfect Customers: The Power of Strategic Synchronicity[8]** *by Stacey Hall and Jan Brogniez. In this chapter, you will learn more about this classic book and how it can help you.*

I have never thought of myself as a particularly strategic person. I hate to admit that I have made a lot of business decisions without seriously consid-ering any overall strategy. Sure, I've always listed out the positive effects and potential consequences of my options, but then I've chosen paths based mostly on emotions (like fear: I had better take this contract because I don't know if something better might come along).

However, I have changed, partly because I read *Attracting Perfect Custom-ers*[8] with my business book club. The change didn't come easily; I began skeptically. One of my core values is "Progress, not perfection," so the title of the book seemed really wrong to me. I first got hooked on page 12 with their metaphor about a lighthouse standing proud and tall, attracting certain boats with its light, not running up and down the beach to catch the atten-tion of all boat captains. Funny: That was exactly how I was feeling, like I was frantically waving my arms yelling "Hire me!" without much success. My method surely was not working for me.

So I read on. My next revelation was the sentence "… listen to your tiny inner voice, the one that speaks for your instincts, which said, 'Be careful. This one could be more trouble than he's worth. This customer is not meant for you'" (p. 14). Wow! They must have been reading my e-mail! I was still smarting from a disastrous meeting with a client that had ended with her snarling at me: "What part of NO don't you understand?" I submitted my next deliverable and left the project immediately; however, I was still "grinding" on what had gone wrong.

Accepting the teaching

Okay. I felt like I needed this book, so I sat down and vowed to finish it, exercises and all, within a day or two, and I did! I'm not going to review the book or the exercises exhaustively, but rather tell you what I learned and how it has affected my independent practice—and might affect yours.

One exercise, the "Strategic Attraction Planning Process," asked me to write down answers to four questions about my perfect customer: Questions 1, 2, and 3 asked about the qualities, motivations, and expectations of my perfect customer. Question 4 prompted me to think about what I need to do to adapt to my client's needs (p. 65).

My strategic attraction plan

(Please note: I haven't listed all the items in any part of my strategic attraction plan, just the ones that might help explain this process better.)

To answer Question 1, I envisioned my perfect customer (for one of my service lines, I teach technical writing in corporations). I chose Remmele Engineering in St. Paul, Minnesota, where I had taught for ten years. Here are a few of their perfect qualities:

1. Their management and employees treated me like an expert who could provide answers to their persistent problems.
2. They funded my research on their behalf (focus groups with their employees).
3. They provided every resource I asked for and offered even more.
4. Their management supported me in the face of some minor resistance from their employees.
5. The managers attended my classes with the employees and provided valuable feedback.
6. They paid promptly.

7. They contracted with me to evaluate each individual's writing and to meet in person with each individual learner.

8. They asked me to identify people who needed the most help and then paid me to coach those individuals.

But here is my best "perfect customer" anecdote: One year I kidded my contact that since we had booked a class on my birthday, they should pay me double (he knew I was joking). However, as a surprise on my birthday, they delivered an immense, creamy-delicious birthday cake and invited all my past students in the company to celebrate. They took pictures and even hugged me (remember, they're engineers).

It was easy to select them as my perfect customer. I moved on to Question 2: What makes my perfect customer tick? It was valuable to articulate what I thought about them: They believe they can solve problems, grow in their understanding of their jobs, see progress; they are engineers, after all. They wanted me to explain, in numbers, the return-on-investment for communication skills. They wanted facts, not just my opinions. And they wanted it all in a fast-paced, hands-on, practical environment.

Question 3 was fun: I listed all the services that my perfect customer might expect me to deliver or provide. This included online drill and practice for grammar and punctuation improvement, webinars for geographically dispersed teams, e-mail tips on better writing habits, online assessments of writing and grammar skills, and a style guide. My customer hadn't asked for these yet, but I wanted to provide these services to them.

Question 4 asked me what I needed to improve to attract or maintain my perfect relationships with my perfect customers. Immediately, I listed that I needed a vehicle to deliver an online course, I needed to learn how to provide webinars, and I had to find an online testing and assessment service.

The rewards

I completed my plan in mid-July 2004. Later that month, I proposed a webinar to the Society for Technical Communication (STC)[1] and was hired

---

[1] http://www.stc.org

to deliver my first webinar, allowing me to practice in a medium I hadn't delivered in before. In August 2004, I stumbled across an online testing and assessment service and contracted with them to provide me with three tests and three surveys concurrently. That November, a client at Remmele asked me to assess potential employees' writing skills as a part of the company's hiring practice. I had the online testing in place and could meet their needs immediately. I also moved ahead with an online delivery platform for more drill and practice, and again, Remmele offered to pay for this service. I spent the next year actively working on all the other services I listed in answering Question 4 for future delivery. In essence, I was extending or "telescoping" my skills (see Chapter 7, *Telescoping for Survival*).

It's important to mention here that all of these good things just flowed to me. I didn't struggle at all for any of them. These opportunities presented themselves, and having completed my plan, I recognized their potential value and selected them as perfect for me at the moment. I don't understand it, I can't explain it, and I won't defend its blatantly spiritual component against a skeptic. I just know to my core that I am different now that I follow this path and that my satisfaction with my business is much, much higher.

More gratitude

Another benefit of working the exercises was a four-page strategic plan that I review regularly (Hall and Brogniez say once a day, but once a week or so is about all I can manage). This reminds me of what I'm trying to accomplish; it's easy to lose sight of any plan without a periodic review.

I've also found that focusing on what makes my customers tick has helped me to understand what makes me tick as a customer. Just as I have been changing to recognize and perform perfect service for my customers, I have been observing my own vendors' service more carefully. Those who provide the best service earn my loyalty. I now write many more "thank yous"—for example, I recently moved all my communications (at least eight components) to one company. My salesperson, Daryl, followed up again and again through this torturous process, interceding where useful. The new company generally offers better service than my old providers (although a far cry from "perfect" service nonetheless), but my salesperson was an impeccable example of perfect service. I sent two letters of commendation, one to Daryl's supervisor and another to that person's supervisor, just because it made me feel great to recognize his excellent efforts.

Likewise, I have been conscious of providing perfect service to Remmele. One of my learners couldn't make it to the regular one-on-one sessions because he was on vacation. In the past, I would have been irritated to have to travel to meet with him at his convenience. However, perfect service should meet his needs, not mine, and my cheerful cooperation and flexibility were verbally recognized by management (who, by the way, then bought refresher courses and updates for all employees. I welcomed this continued income stream.)

Another huge benefit of having this particular strategic plan is a deeper awareness that not all customers are perfect customers; therefore, losing certain business is a blessing. Remember the customer who snarled at me? She wanted me to cut corners at every turn; she questioned every 15 minutes I spent on creating an instructional design for her; and she demeaned virtually every statement I made. Unfortunately, this contract represented about $30,000 of potential business. Ouch! It was hard to trust my instincts that not only was she NOT a perfect customer, she was already a nightmare customer and we had only just begun our relationship. I had to let go and trust that better customers would come along, and of course, they have.

A word if you are newly independent: You may not have past experience with perfect customers, but you can certainly imagine a perfect customer based on your past work experience. After all, you have had customers in past jobs (your supervisor, co-workers, and other employees). Create personas from these people and experiences as you work through the exercises in the book until you actually have customers.

I am glad that I have begun to think more strategically in my business. I certainly feel more at peace with my decisions and the path of my business. I still have to market to attract perfect customers (because in real life, customers may disappear for many reasons), but now I know how to recognize potential perfect customers so that my efforts are more productive today than ever before.

CHAPTER 5

Prospecting for Your Perfect Customer

There's gold in the ground, and there's gold in your marketplace, if only you can unearth it. This chapter uses the analogy of prospecting for gold to show you how you could strategically develop your customer base and find your perfect customer (as explained in Chapter 4, Attracting Perfect Customers). Independents who don't market well, including mastering the skill of prospecting, often become employees again. Use the skills below to increase your income and guarantee your success as an independent.

Consider this short historical anecdote with direct relevance to your income:

> ...in the Sacramento Valley of California one frosty January morning in 1848, an itinerant carpenter who was putting up a sawmill on the South Fork of the American River for Johann Augustus Sutter saw something gleaming in the bottom of the new millrace, picked it up, found another, and exclaimed to his fellow workers, "Boys, I think I have found a gold mine."
>
> By the end of that year, no less than $6 million in the yellow metal had been won by the early stampeders. (p. 10)
> —Bradford Angier, *Looking for Gold: The Modern Prospector's Handbook*[2]

So it is with the marketing practices of independent consultants. You, too, could stumble over a "gold mine" and find your perfect customer. Of course, like the carpenter in the story above, you would have to be "out there" to find this customer. The carpenter would never have discovered gold while loitering at the saloon; likewise, you will not uncover the perfect customer by sitting in your office.

Prospecting is a crucial strategic business skill for independents. This chapter will focus on using prospecting methods, including cold calls, to increase your customer base and your income. If the term "cold call" gives you the shivers, please don't skip this chapter just yet! I'll show you how cold calls can increase your income substantially. Remember, it was winter when Sutter discovered gold, and most prospectors worked year-round. Working outside your comfort zone can help you reap rewards. I know personally that prospecting is effective: In some years, I have earned over 50 percent of my income as the direct result of deliberate prospecting, and I'm as marketing-phobic as you are.

Determine your perfect customer

To decide what type of customer is perfect for you, go through your current and past customer list and rank all your customers. If you want to be thorough, follow the strategic exercises in *Attracting Perfect Customers*[8]. When I did these exercises for my business (I help create better writers through classes and coaching, and I also edit medical documents), I discovered that two engineering firms were my best customers. I realized that they always seemed to appreciate my expertise, were easy to deal with, provided every resource I requested, paid me well and fast, and didn't quibble over nickels. I feel I am collaborating with them, and I feel energized by my work with them. Employees at these companies stay in touch by e-mailing intelligent and interesting comments and questions. I always want to hear from them, and I always want to go back to teach them and others at their companies.

If you're new to independent consulting, you might have to use your imagination to project your perfect customer in order to get your prospecting off the ground. Perhaps you can base your projections on personas of perfect customers from former employers, or you might be able to interview some experienced freelancers about the qualities of their perfect customers to establish a persona for your prospecting.

Prospect to find new candidates

Just as gold prospectors had to do, I must go where I might find gold. Armed with the names of my perfect customers, I begin by searching any resource that lists all the companies in my geographic area of choice. I use my local business library, where I can get free access to ReferenceUSA®.[1] You could also use print-based texts that list companies by number of employees; annual sales; location (ZIP code or metropolitan area); and NAICS (North American Industry Classification Systems).[2]

I first search for my existing perfect customers. I find their number of employees, NAICS code, and annual sales. Here's what appears in the database for my perfect customer, the engineering firm:

1. 300-500 employees at one site
2. Sales of over $30,000,000
3. NAICS code range

Then I use this information as parameters for finding similar companies in the database. If the initial list produced from these parameters is too short, I might drop the sales parameter. For example, when I searched on variables of 300-500 employees, $30,000,000 in sales, within 30 ZIP codes near my home, I located 1,975 companies. It is easy to narrow or enlarge the search by adjusting parameters.

Once I have finalized the list, I save it into a spreadsheet. I study the list. What companies have I heard of before? What companies are in my Potential File (where I store newspaper articles for future reference)? Whom do I know from my network who works for one of these potential customers? What can they tell me that I could add to the spreadsheet? What have I heard (negative or positive) about this company from my wider network or on the business page of my local paper? Can I mine information from the company's website or from articles in business newsletters or journals?

Contact prospects

Now I think about my current customers again. What are the titles of my contacts? I usually contract my training through the HR manager or director, although larger companies might refer to these positions as training

---

[1] Find ReferenceUSA at a library near you: http://referenceusa.com/Static/LibraryLocator

[2] http://www.census.gov/eos/www/naics/codes (federal government designations of primary product or industry).

manager or director. For my editing clients, I look for clinical research managers or directors. Your typical contact might be a marketing director or technical support director, depending on your product or service line.

Finally, I call each prospective company's general phone number (listed in referenceUSA or on the company's website) to get the name of a potential contact: "Hello! I need the name of your training manager." Notice that I use the verb *need*. I have found that people often respond favorably to a need rather than a want.

Keep a positive attitude about your mission. Freelancers may be shy and introverted. I know that I hated making these calls—until I started seeing the gold (er, contracts) flow in. I try to reframe the situation in self-talk: "I have a great skill I can share to serve these companies and improve their business practices." Given that fact, it is only natural that I would need the name of a contact person to begin the process and that I would ask for it.

It is true that I occasionally find a receptionist who doesn't cooperate, but it only happens less than 1 percent of the time. Remember that gold prospectors didn't give up and go away just because one site was unproductive.

Usually, the receptionist will look through the company directory and give me the name of my potential contact. They often offer to connect me with this individual, and if I actually get them on the phone, I am prepared with my thirty-second infomercial (elevator speech):

> Hello! This is Bette Frick, and my company is The Text Doctor. I serve companies like yours by helping create better writers through classes, coaching, and editing. I wonder if I could help your company solve some of your communication problems?

Responses vary from "Yes, I'm interested" to "No, thanks, we have perfect writers here" (seriously, it happens). If they are interested, I keep asking questions and try to arrange an appointment. If they say no, I ask if I can send them my latest newsletter or a postcard with my latest offering. Be sure to have some marketing materials ready to pop in the mail that day.

If I reach them only through their voicemail, I leave my contact information and mail them a postcard or newsletter. I follow up a week later to see if they received my mailing and ask if I can answer any questions.

What I've just accomplished is a cold call, defined as a personal visit or telephone call to someone you don't know for the purpose of selling them something. A variation is the *warm* call, where you have a contact inside or outside the company who has allowed you to use his or her name as a reference. There's no doubt that warm calls are easier to make, but you probably will still need to make cold calls. Remember, prospectors often worked in the cold.

To improve your performance, memorize and rehearse your script, improvising slightly different deliveries in case you get a live person who asks questions. I have found it very effective to practice with other independents in my network—just ask a few independents with whom you enjoy interacting if they would like to practice cold calling with you. I have done that myself and it has always been a valuable experience that forms a good relationship with other independents.

You may be groaning by now, muttering "This is awful work! This takes so much time!" Yes, you are right, but before you give up, let's look at another historical example of gold prospecting mentioned in Angier's book:

> A wrong measurement on Bonanza Creek left open a slab of land 86 feet broad at its widest spot. Dick Lowe, a chain man on a survey crew, decided to stake it after failing to find a larger fraction. He had no luck in selling it for $900 or even leasing it, so he dug a shaft himself. Nothing! He tried again, and this time washed out $46,000 in eight hours. The tiny pie-shaped wedge finally gave up half a million dollars. (p. 12)

Remember, it's not about YOU; it's about THE NUMBERS. The more calls you make, the more negatives you will get, but it takes a certain number of NOs to get a "YES, I'd love to meet you and find out what you can offer us." Perhaps I am lucky that I once sold real estate and learned to make cold calls 30 years ago. Back then, my manager preached that every negative response was bringing me closer to a yes answer.

You might need to bribe yourself to make cold calls. I divide my calls into blocks of ten and treat myself to something special after each block: a walk in the woods with my dog, a special meal, a nice hot bath, a new book, or shopping therapy. Whatever it takes, I keep digging.

You may find yourself becoming negative in the face of rejection (it happens!). Post a list of affirmations from your customers. My list includes a picture of the beautiful cake that my perfect engineering company delivered to my classroom while I was training on my birthday. All the engineers that I had taught came by to feast during our break. Now, that's a perfect customer—one who appreciates me as much as I appreciate them. If there's one perfect customer in my list, there must be others out there too. This positive interlude helps me keep mining my list.

Continue to contact prospects

Contact enough companies in your list, and you will get another, smaller list of live prospects. They usually won't "buy" the first time you contact them; in fact, it is important to know and remember that prospects generally need an average of seven contacts before they are ready to purchase.

So you will need to prepare yourself to keep on mining for a contract. Like other independents, I produce a newsletter (mostly information, very little marketing) to e-mail to contacts. If you have updated your website, you could send a postcard inviting contacts to visit the newly designed site. Or, as you read the business section of your local newspaper, you might notice that a prospect's stock is up or they just received FDA approval for a new drug or device. Drop them a card recognizing their company's achievement. Each contact is moving you closer to the average of seven needed to convert a prospect to a sale.

Dig in for the long haul

If you stick with it, prospecting can uncover shiny new contracts. In this last historical quote, Angier illustrates the payoff of patience:

Three Australians …bought a 12-month lease on Beach No. Two in Nome.
[They] nearly ran out of money unsuccessfully working it but agreed to continue.…[they] got down to their last day of funds when they found gravel and
sand glittering with gold at the bottom of their shaft and took out $413,000
in gold during their last 30 days. (p. 10)

I love sales that drop into my lap as a result of networking (see Chapter 21,
Networking for Independents), but the sweetest sales I make are the ones
I've prospected for. In fact, customers whom I have found through prospecting have stayed with me the longest, for some reason. It might be that I
work harder to serve customers I worked so hard to find.

Perseverance makes the difference between prospectors and everyone else.
According to Dean Littlepage, author of *Gold Fever in the North: The Alaska-
Yukon Gold Rush Era*[11] and guest curator of a special exhibit in the An-
chorage Museum of History and Art, the era of the Alaska-Yukon Gold
Rush (1896) "was a time when ordinary people did extraordinary things."
Most of the gold stampeders were ordinary people driven to Alaska by
economic conditions in the lower 48. One such miner was asked the secret
of his luck. He replied, "Just digging holes."

CHAPTER 6
Are You a Generalist or a Specialist? Focusing Your Business

As you strategize your freelance business, you will need to decide whether you will generalize or specialize. Liz Willis,[1] my personal editor, helped write this chapter, in which we present six tips for focusing your business strategically.

Is it better for a freelancer to be a generalist or a specialist? That's a perennial question among freelancers—and plenty of other professionals, too. And while it makes a fascinating topic for debate, it's far too big a question for one chapter. So, here's a variation on the theme: If you are an incurable generalist, can you still enjoy some of the advantages enjoyed by specialists? The answer is yes.

Both Liz and I consider ourselves generalists, and we are betting that a sizable percentage of independents do, too. How do we define generalist? We love variety, we love to learn, and we love to think (we both have "Learner" and "Intellection" as our Signature Strengths as identified by Strengths Finder 2.0,[2]). Liz likes to write and edit, and I like to teach writing and to edit. We both find the notion of limiting ourselves to a narrow subject area or discipline dreary and uninspiring.

But for independents, being a generalist has potential drawbacks, one of the biggest being lack of focus. What, exactly, do you want to do, and for whom? If you are unable to answer these basic questions, you may have trouble attracting business. A focused freelancer inspires confidence. At the very least, you will need to determine your strengths, define the market for your services, and position yourself within that market.

---

[1] http://www.lizwillis.com/
[2] http://www.strengthsfinder.com/home.aspx

And don't forget to create a list of standards that includes the kind of projects you will do and the high-quality clients you would work for (and those whom you might not work for—see Chapter 9, *The Best Job I Never Took*).

And speaking of high-quality clients, finding and retaining clients who treat you well and whose values and working style mesh well with yours is also critical—and another way of focusing your business. In *Attracting Perfect Customers: The Power of Strategic Synchronicity*[8], the authors invite us to define who is, or would be, a perfect customer for us and to tailor our offerings to meet their needs.

Two paths toward greater focus

I am a good example of a generalist who has specialized successfully. When I first started my business, I offered writing, editing, and training services. Once I discovered that I loved training and that it paid well, I focused my business in that area. Later, when the economy soured and training budgets were slashed (a normal cycle in business, I have found), I added medical editing to my offerings, a decision made easier when one of my key training clients asked me to edit as well. I love the new mix and the fact that I'm learning something new every day.

Liz offers writing, editing, and proofreading services to a variety of clients. Although her work has been well received, she is concerned that her business lacks focus. Luckily, positive experiences on some recent Web projects, including one that involves writing and editing career- and job-search-related content, have suggested that a closer focus on Web content might be a logical next step. Among her goals were to update her website to reflect her increasing interest in Web-based projects; continue to improve her copywriting skills; and explore books and possibly a course on taxonomy, a discipline that would satisfy her generalist sensibilities while offering another possible area of focus.

Six tips for focusing your business

While there are no strict rules for focusing your business, there are some basic guidelines you can follow. Whether you have been in business for a while or are just starting out, we hope you will benefit from these tips:

1. Figure out what you love to do and what you do well. Invest in whatever tools you need to help you figure this out. We both like *Strengths Finder 2.0*[13], which gave us great insight into our motivated skills and personality traits. Many books for freelancers and small-business owners offer excellent advice on self-assessment and defining your business (see the Resource List[3]).

2. Once you know what you want to do, commit to it. Don't just think about it, take action. For example, when I decided to focus on training, I joined the American Society for Training and Development (ASTD),[4] created professional training materials, and promoted this service line through networking and marketing. I have made similar efforts through the American Medical Writers Association (AMWA)[5] as I market my medical editing services to prospective clients.

3. Identify your ideal client. Specialize in clients who offer the work you want, respect you as a professional, and pay you well. While this seems self-evident, both of us have worked in situations where that wasn't the case. Yes, you will often need to take assignments just to pay the bills, but striving to find clients with whom you are compatible should be a top goal.

4. Educate yourself continuously. Continuing education is not only critical for establishing credibility, it also helps you further define what you want to do. As I pursued training and certification through AMWA and the Board of Editors in the Life Sciences (BELS),[6] I constantly gained insights on my skills and abilities. The Society for Technical Communication (STC) offers a certification program[7] that provides similar opportunities as well.

---

[3] http://www.textdoctor.com/bizresources
[4] http://www.astd.org/
[5] http://www.amwa.org
[6] http://www.bels.org/
[7] http://www.stc.org/education/certification/certification-main

5. Offer closely related services. Offering related services allows you to achieve variety but still have control over your marketing and educational efforts. It's also a way to leverage your investments. For example, the work I have done to educate myself to specialize in medical editing is helping me further refine my training services for my med-tech clients. (For examples of freelancers who have productively offered closely related services, see Chapter 7, *Telescoping for Survival*.)

6. Be open to new experiences. Opportunities will arise that you didn't necessarily plan for, but being open to change is critical to success. When one of my med-tech training clients asked me to edit their medical materials, I accepted the offer. Editing is now one of my key services and one that I enjoy immensely.

When it comes to focusing your business, the tips above just barely scratch the surface. And, as we mentioned earlier, the specialist-vs-generalist debate is a complex topic that we don't have room to fully explore here. For more on the debate and how generalists can thrive in a specialist world, check out Freelance Folder,[8] an online community for independents. In a discussion titled "Do You Need to Specialize to Succeed?"[9] participants tackle the issue head-on and also discuss frequent stereotypes and misconceptions.

We believe that to succeed as a generalist and an independent, you don't need to change who you are (nor should you try), but you do need to find ways to define your business. Some of that will come through self-assessment, some through training and education, and some through serendipity and openness to new opportunities.

Of course, figuring all this out takes time; it won't happen overnight. Expect plenty of trial and error as you strive to discover the ideal combination of services and clients. The main thing is to just get started. As we learned in Chapter 5, *Prospecting for Your Perfect Customer*, successful prospectors staked their claims and worked them hard. If at first they didn't succeed, they moved on to work another claim.

---

[8] http://freelancefolder.com/
[9] http://freelancefolder.com/freelance-specialist-vs-generalist/

CHAPTER 7

Telescoping for Survival

Standard business advice for small businesses is to specialize in good economic times and "telescope" (extend your services) when corporations are tightening their belts. In this chapter, seasoned freelancers offer their experience with telescoping their services to survive when money is tight.

One of the many advantages of aging is that I've survived several US recessions (1973–75, 1980–1982, 1990–1991, 2001–2003, 2007–2011). I launched The Text Doctor in 1990 after having experienced two layoffs in seven months during that recession.

Unfortunately, my advancing age means that I can barely remember what I did to survive these hard times (only partially kidding here). I do know that in the past, I have personalized the slowdown more than I should have. I just recently reassured a young friend (a video producer) not to take these slow times personally. "We're all struggling a bit…even those of us who have been in business awhile," I said.

In preparation for writing this chapter, I surveyed fellow independents to see what strategies all of us were using to thrive in the Great Recession. I specifically wanted to know more about telescoping, also known as diversification, which involves proposing and delivering additional services to your favorite or best clients. The advantage to your clients is that they know and trust you and do not have to go through extensive vetting of another vendor and building another relationship; the advantage to you is that you generate additional revenue without extensive marketing costs and you will stretch yourself to learn and deliver new services.

Twenty-two independents responded and nineteen completed the survey. Nearly three-quarters of us (72.7%) telescoped our offerings to survive the last recession, and this chapter shares what we did to expand our services and how we are doing that. I will share freelancers' concerns with the process and conclude with some hopeful stories.

What freelancers have done to telescope

Katherine Noftz Nagel (Masterwork Consulting)[1] offered training to her documentation and online help clients and site maintenance to web design clients. Mindy Hoffbauer (Write Angle Consulting)[2] expanded into marcomm (marketing communications), corporate communications, branding, corporate identity, and public relations. Yet another training and coaching specialist added writing as an additional service line; another added proposals, grant applications, and publicity.

Beryl Gray shared, "I added greatly increased options for document delivery. Where I usually provide source files and printable files, I now include file (or paper) delivery to a prepress agency, printer, or the customer's customer. I try to anticipate what value I would have desired as a customer of a writing consultant."

Andrea C. Carrero (Word Technologies)[3] added: "I have broadened my services to offer marketing and other business-related communication services. I am a former journalist, have done public relations, and have a wealth of publication experience behind me, in addition to a really deep technical knowledge. This allows me to offer a wide variety of services to a wide variety of clients."

Screencasting has helped Holly Mullins (Instructive Media)[4] to offer her clients screencast demos and tutorials as a service line, and she continued to work to expand her services in e-learning into the biomedical communication field.

How independents expand services

During the recession, independents learned new tools, got certifications, offered classes, joined new professional organizations, networked endlessly, became more visible through leadership roles, and revisited former market segments.

---

[1] http://www.masterworkconsulting.com/
[2] http://www.writeangle.biz/
[3] http://www.wordtex.com/
[4] http://instructivemedia.com

Some freelancers have updated their skills by adding skills in creative tools such as Dreamweaver® and InDesign® so that they could offer clients consistent content that works for both print and online media. Likewise, another freelancer acquired training for the Project Management Professional (PMP) certification and plans to complete the PMP exam.

Ginny Redish of Redish & Associates Inc.[5] offered: "Twice recently, I gave a workshop on writing for the web for a client where I made a point of putting the idea into the client's mind that I could also help by mentoring content writers individually. Both clients have now come back to me and asked for that service."

Some of us diversified our memberships in professional organizations to increase our contacts and specialties. One freelancer joined her Chamber of Commerce to get to know small- and medium-sized business owners. She then volunteered her services as the marketing and communications committee chairperson, which has opened doors to working with other communications professionals, extending her professional network, and finding new work within the membership. She found that her big investment of time and energy was well worth the effort.

Networking never goes out of style, according to Mindy Hoffbauer: "I never quit networking. In both good times and not so good, I continue to network everywhere I go: at STC (Society for Technical Communication) meetings, charity events, on my kids' soccer field, through my volunteering activities…I've never had to go looking for work."

Leadership roles are invaluable long-term assets in stabilizing income, as Linda Gallagher of TechCom Plus LLC[6] shared: "It helps to have been around for 20 years and have taken visible leadership roles, mostly in STC. Of course, I do have lulls, but my income has remained fairly stable over many years."

Gray suggested: "I have revisited market segments in which I have previously worked but left for more profitable (or more comfortable) segments."

---

[5] http://www.redish.net/
[6] http://techcomplus.com/

Concerns about telescoping

Lyn Worthen of Information Design Co.[7] cautioned freelancers not to use telescoping as a crisis-management tool: "While the idea of 'telescoping' isn't a bad one, too many people will suddenly try to offer additional services during lean times that they haven't refined when times were more stable. As a result, they can actually end up causing their reputation damage. If you have a strong skill that you're not currently offering (maybe it's not your favorite thing, or an area you find you've not worked in for a while, but still are still competent in), sure, extend your services in that area to increase your chances of staying employed during lean times. But don't decide to pick up a new skill and try to market it now, out of desperation."

Gallagher claimed that she's "...not really comfortable and get[s] rather stressed by trying to be a marketing writer or article author or other type of writer that is outside what I know I'm good at." Another independent worried that a tight economy might not be the best time to sell a new service.

Some hopeful telescoping stories

An unidentified respondent shared a very positive experience with telescoping: "I am a copyeditor/proofreader. A current client asked if I could help with ad copy, and I replied that it was not my area of expertise, but that I was willing to do whatever it took to get the job done. It worked out well! I did consult with another coworker whose specialty is marketing communications. She gave me her quick-and-dirty 20-minute lesson in how to write ad copy. I followed suit and my client was very pleased. Oh, I think I got lucky, too!"

Another anonymous contributor said: "I'm a freelance technical writer and have been working with one client for the past four years. This client had a layoff in November and has since asked me to write product specifications and marketing brochures in addition to keeping the documents current. I'm really enjoying the change of pace and the opportunity to prove how valuable I can be to this client."

---

[7] http://www.infodesignco.com/?page_id=39

Tony Chung[8] wrote of the exhilaration of telescoping: "I took on some web design and programming contracts that are still keeping me busy even though I've started a new full-time writing contract. Things are getting exciting because I have also been asked to flex my artistic and multimedia muscles, further telescoping into other areas of interest that I've always wanted to explore."

Try. Fail? Try again.

Two quotes continue to inspire me as I think strategically about my business:

- "The best way to predict the future is to invent it." (Alan Kay)
- "Try again. Fail again. Fail better." (Samuel Beckett)

Respondents to the survey appeared to agree with these sentiments. Hoffbauer said, "The only time I experience personal or professional growth is when I push the envelope. Telescoping can sometimes involve stepping outside our comfort zones, but it always pays off."

An anonymous responder summarized this discussion: "The essential law of economics as well as nature is that we must adapt to conditions as opposed to standing still and hoping that conditions change to make our present situation relevant. In the current economy, businesses are working to become leaner, so all professionals who want to stay employed must adapt to add value to their organizations. The same goes for freelancers. This is nothing new."

Adversity may be the springboard for doing something you did not plan. Sudden change can be a real gift for freelancers if it leads to new growth.

---

[8] http://tonychung.ca/

CHAPTER 8
Medical Writing and Editing Opportunities for Freelancers

In the last chapter, Chapter 7, Telescoping for Survival, we explored how you can expand your service lines to survive in a recession. In this chapter, I will share how I telescoped my services into a profitable and enjoyable medical editing business.

As The Text Doctor LLC, I "doctor" (edit) medical texts. I am unable to doctor humans because the sight of blood makes me queasy. In spite of this career-limiting defect, I am glad that I was eventually able to migrate into medical editing after years of teaching technical writing in medical manufacturing firms.

It was relatively easy to transfer my editing skills and knowledge into the medical field; after all, editing is editing, regardless of the subject. What wasn't easy was learning the new vocabulary, facts, principles, and concepts about medicine that form the basis of knowledge in the medical field. However, I found many exciting opportunities to learn more in this and related fields.

Credentials can lead to success

Shortly after I began editing medical documents, I joined the American Medical Writers Association (AMWA).[1] In many ways, AMWA resembles the Society for Technical Communication (STC)[2] and other professional societies and organizations. It provides members with listservs, online resources, publications, an annual conference, and educational opportunities.

---

[1] http://www.amwa.org/
[2] http://www.stc.org/

I enrolled in the AMWA Essential Skills (ES) certificate program, which consists of eight rigorous, graded courses. All courses in the first certificate can now be completed by self-study. I completed the ES certificate in November 2010 and continued studying for advanced certificates at annual conferences.

I also studied and passed the Board of Editors in the Life Sciences examination (BELS)[3] to formalize and extend my knowledge of medical editing. Studying for both the AMWA and BELS certification programs revealed a vast pool of "unknown unknowns," and I spent at least a year learning facts and concepts that now inform my editing. (In addition to my deliberate avoidance of blood, I had always shunned numbers, statistics, and scientific study—the very basis of medical writing and editing. I had a lot to learn!)

Telescoping can also lead to success

For me, the benefits of launching into the medical field have been a steady source of excellent clients; the field of medicine is expanding, growing, and changing all the time. The documents that I edit are fascinating and perhaps even life-saving. Potential work can be found in many different venues:

- Pharmaceutical companies
- Medical manufacturing companies
- Scientific and medical communication agencies
- Medical education and communications companies
- Clinical research organizations
- Universities and medical schools
- Hospitals and clinics
- Associations, publishers, and journals

The health and medical sectors of our economy will continue to grow. Could these sectors provide a potential market for you? If you like reading consumer materials about health, perhaps you could explore writing health-related articles. From there, you might market your skills to the many

---

[3] http://www.bels.org/becomeeditor/index.htm

contract research organizations and consulting firms throughout the country. Visit a local AMWA chapter meeting if you can. Consider attending the AMWA annual conference to learn more about writing and editing in this field. I think you will find the basic principles of technical writing you have already learned from membership in STC or other professional organizations will be supported and enhanced by membership and participation in several organizations.

Plan on investing time and money into constant learning in these fields.

I chose medical editing as opposed to medical writing because I wanted to remain a generalist rather than a specialist. (See Chapter 6, *Are You a Generalist or a Specialist? Focusing Your Business.*) Medical writers seem to specialize in a field such as oncology, cardiovascular, or pharmacology more than editors do. In the past week, I have edited five articles for a private healthcare database for cost and quality managers; a proposal to offer counseling services to the federal government; and pages for a medical manufacturing website. Next week, I might be editing a clinical submission. No two projects, documents, or clients are the same, and I am constantly stretching my brain to learn new technologies and terminology. If you like learning and are excited about helping people through your work, consider consulting and contracting in the medical field.

CHAPTER 9
The Best Job I Never Took

Most freelancers have accepted work that ultimately turned out to be financially non-productive and psychologically difficult, often because they were feeling financially insecure, even desperate. Most of us have regretted taking "bad" jobs. This chapter shares some disaster stories and provides hope that you can trust your intuition to turn down certain contracts.

My father was a gambling man, reformed by my mother to playing poker with his buddies only once a month. One way he dealt with his poker deprivation was to teach us poker, which led to many intensely competitive evenings of playing poker for quarters with my brothers. Bless my father—he always tried to tell me when to "fold" my cards (to realize when my hand was so bad that I couldn't and shouldn't continue to play). I never really understood what he was trying to teach me until I was in business for myself and had to reject projects that I desperately wanted to take on or keep for the income that I needed.

This chapter will explore the reasoning process behind the decisions that independents and other technical communicators make in accepting or rejecting potential paid work. Please note: I'm not writing about decisions we all make at the beginning of our career or business. Most of us take on early work and working relationships without the luxury of being able to say "No, not at this time." When I first opened shop, I took any and every contract that came along, grateful for the work then and grateful now for all those learning experiences.

As I look back on my freelance career, I see that selectivity as a business strategy has helped save me time, stress, and money. I first subscribed to the concept of selectivity when I read *Attracting Perfect Customers: The Power of Strategic Synchronicity*[8]. This workbook asked me to list all the qualities of my best client and then think about accepting only similar clients in the future. (See Chapter 4, *Attracting Perfect Customers: Developing Your Strategic Plan.*)

What impressed me most in the book *Attracting Perfect Customers* was the suggestion that we all have a "tiny inner voice, the one that speaks for your instincts, which [can say to us], 'Be careful. This one could be more trouble than he's worth. This customer is not meant for you'" (p. 14).

This advice struck home, as I had recently experienced a disastrous client relationship that went bad right at the start. Looking back, I can now see the warning signs that I didn't understand then: This new client had questioned every line item on my bid, trying to get me to lower the price without reducing deliverables. That should have alerted me to a problem right away. By contrast, my "perfect customers" never questioned my very reasonable bids; when I provided them with options, they usually selected quality over cost and showed respect for my suggestions at every decision point. Every new contract with these perfect customers proceeded to a good conclusion and more work.

Learning to recognize warning signs

After studying the message of *Attracting Perfect Customers*, I used my new-found intuition to decline work. I was asked to teach writing to the employees of a public works department of a local city. The director disparaged the writing of his employees but could not share any specific examples. I asked to interview a few of the writers, who told me that the director read every word of their communication and demanded changes in their texts based on his own quirky writing standards—then he rewrote their revised texts back to their original version!

The three employees I interviewed were frustrated almost to tears. I asked them if they thought the director would be open to coaching or suggestions, or even might attend the class. They had no hope for such an intervention. I declined to pursue the contract because I recognized how emotionally charged the classroom could become and how ineffective I would be in changing this dysfunctional situation or helping these people write better under the circumstances. Although I would have liked the revenue from this contract and further business with this city, I felt that it was not going to be worth it.

Other freelancers recognize warning signs

Alice Jane Emanuel,[1] who lives in the Netherlands, shared a similar story:

A few weeks ago, I interviewed for something that looked great on paper: They would meet my current salary, they offered decent benefits, and the position was technically challenging.

The warning signs started to show up immediately with my first impression of the company: a chaotic and dirty office space. The person interviewing me, who would be my boss, said he would be changing jobs within the company soon but that he did not know what he would be doing. "For now, assume I would be your boss." Fine.

We discussed the company. He mentioned they would soon relocate to a larger open-plan office situation. They would be closer to the railway station and he would expect "eight more minutes of productivity per employee per day." The co-interviewer, an exhausted-looking corporate communication manager, met my eyes in one of those dead stares that said, "Just don't react." Nothing I can't handle, maybe, but I'm starting to get an unpleasant feeling about the company.

Both interviewers then began to describe the man who would be my chief subject matter expert. "Can you work with difficult people?" they asked. "My entire career," I answered. "Piece of cake." They loosened and described him as "challenging" and "not always easy to work with." I know that it's a Dutch trait to speak plainly so I take this in with ease.

The SME (subject matter expert) entered the interview. We spoke for a few minutes in a relaxed way and he mentioned that he brought material along to explain his product's technology. "No other so-called technical writer has been able to understand it," he said. I asked to see it. He reared back, "I'm not used to being bossed around by a candidate!" It really was almost a shout. I smiled but did not otherwise react.

At that point I realized I could not possibly take the position. To do so would be to fight every single working day just to be able to do my job. It was a blow, but I comfort myself when I scan the job postings: That company is still looking for someone.

---

[1] http://commatheory.com/

Suzanne Guess (210 Communications[2]) had an experience that taught her how to recognize warning signs of impending disaster:

> A direct mail supplier in town wanted graphic design services as well as freelance writing, and I have resources for both. We signed a contract and started work, but I could not nail him down on requirements (warning sign #1). Soon, he was calling me at night and on weekends. When I didn't answer, he would call my staff directly (he called the graphic designer at 2 am), even though our agreement was to work through me (warning sign #2). After 5 weeks, he still had not paid the 30% down payment (warning sign #3). When I talked to him about it, he became verbally abusive (warning sign #4). After that conversation, I checked my state's online court records (strategy #1) and found that several companies had sued his company for non-payment—and won. The next day, I called him and exercised the clause that allowed me to get out of the contract without any repercussions but still sue for services provided (strategy #2). I followed up with a letter, and then sued him in small claims court (strategy #3).

> What it really boils down to is that I started to realize that he was sucking a disproportionate amount of energy based on the contract dollar amount he brought in. And then there was the verbal abuse not only to me but to the people who work with me. Having their loyalty is far more valuable than any dollar from him.

Thea Teich (Teich Technical and Marketing Communications[3]) suggests charging more as an alternative to turning down the difficult client. Thea describes a very difficult client, suggesting that "a Madame D [code name] project could lead to incipient ulcers, headaches, eyestrain, and extreme frustration....Only one [colleague] is still working on projects for Madame D. And, while I don't know exactly how much this writer is charging her, I know it's more than what I did. But she's put up with the aggravation factor for a long, long time."

Carol Elkins of A Written Word,[4] still smarting from a "project from hell," believes that having an airtight contract will at least begin to cover the dif-

---

[2] http://210comm.net/
[3] http://www.linkedin.com/pub/thea-teich/0/342/397
[4] http://www.awrittenword.com/

ficulties she encountered on a recent project and may help avoid legal costs
down the road. "It's sometimes hard to read the signs that a client may be
difficult...I'm wired to keep going and hope for the best. In this case, that
didn't serve me well."

Fold your cards? Hold them?

Recognizing when to turn down potential work (knowing when to fold
your cards) will help you spot and keep good work when you see it
(knowing when to hold your cards). Experience teaches us these decisions,
but we could all cut our learning curve by asking questions and relying on
fellow independents for wisdom. I have to admit that I've found it hard to
ask for help; I often feel isolated as an independent.

Recently, I had the positive experience of having a fellow freelancer, Donna
Marino, ask me for advice about a bid she wanted to make on a project she
had never done before.

Part of our interaction was her admission that, "Because of tough financial
times, it seems I'm always willing to cut my rates, but I know that's a bad
idea. Then I feel resentful for doing work at lower rates than everyone else.
It's not a good cycle and I've been trying to break it. It's just that when I
can't find work, some money seems better than none."

Together, Donna and I walked through the work required (a lot) and the
money offered (not enough). Then, she wrote, "Well, now I'm having
second (third?) thoughts. This is a sticky situation because a friend referred
me and I'm concerned that I'll impact his relationship with the client if I
refuse to take the project at this point (he is also concerned about that).
Nothing is ever easy, is it?"

Eventually, Donna turned down the work and immediately received another,
more lucrative contract from another client. It was wonderful to be a part
of the discussion, to recognize the need that we all have to keep working
and making money, and to watch someone else choose the right path and
be rewarded for it.

Once we have learned our own priceless lessons of knowing when to turn down a project or leave one midstream, we can share our learning with others. We will all advance in our careers through this valuable process and improve our individual and company performance.

CHAPTER 10
Consulting for Your Local Government

When thinking strategically about your target market, don't forget to consider local government (city, county, or state). I have found lucrative and enjoyable work, often close to home, and a refreshing environment of pleasant public servants. It's even better if you can work for your own city, county, or state government: as a taxpayer, you might even feel increased motivation to help them and save your own tax dollars!

How many times every year do you drive by your city hall? County seat? State government buildings?

I used to park across from our city hall every day when I picked up my mail at the post office. Then I would sweep by the capitol of Minnesota as I drove the freeways in St. Paul. And most of the time, I had the wrong ideas in my head as I passed all these government buildings.

I always thought about how much those government agencies cost me—not how much they might pay me! I was ignoring a whole market sector that has since proved to be a valuable anchor in my portfolio of clients.

The benefits of consulting for the government

There seems to be a stereotype of government work as a joyless, bureaucratic experience. Not so! My experiences have been generally favorable. I have found that my government contracts involved minimal hassle, a relaxed environment, and built-in networking.

Minimal hassle

When I began working for state and local governments in Minnesota, I found several surprises:

- Minnesota's state contracts were easy to understand (written in plain language, no less).
- Bureaucracy, although present, was certainly no worse than at some of my corporate clients.
- The state almost always paid faster and sometimes better than my corporate clients (10 days versus 30 to 60 days or longer). In addition, Minnesota deposits payments automatically into my checking account, saving me a trip to the bank.

Relaxed environment

It's been a joy to collaborate with the employees of my local governments. There seems to be less of an "edge" when working with state or local employees; I find my students and other contacts eager to learn how to do their jobs better without trying to impress an outsider.

As in any workplace, you will find the occasional rigid micromanager, but in general, my state and local clients have been creative, fun, and responsive. My largest contract with the state of Minnesota was not for teaching but for writing and project-managing a broadcast to 40,000-plus employees. In this case, my favorite community college acted as the general contractor and subcontracted with eight other independents to design, develop, and deliver the broadcast. Our clients were respectful of our team's expertise and hosted a modest chocolate party at the end of the project to thank the vendors; by that time, we had all become good friends.

Built-in networking

State employees often move to different departments (sometimes through promotions and sometimes laterally). They don't seem to leave state government, so every move they make gives me increased visibility in their new departments if I maintain contact with them. In addition, my government contacts often network with officials in other government bodies and have provided referrals and recommendations.

How to find local government contacts

If you are lucky, clients or colleagues will have connections—for example, I got started when a client referred me to the Minnesota State Department of Natural Resources for an editing contract. Other work came to me because in Minnesota, the state government uses its community colleges as brokers for many services. Through one contact at one college, I was introduced to several state government departments.

But if you have to do the legwork yourself, there are a number of handy resources available. A Google search will provide you with hours of research possibilities to mine information about your local government officials and contracting possibilities. After I moved to Colorado, I subscribed to a free e-mail alert that sends updates on open bids, archived bids, and contract awards that I could then search on the state website. I could also pay for more extensive bidding information. I also was able to take free classes sponsored by the state to help small businesses navigate the bidding process. There's a lot of free material on the state website: for example, I found the *State of Colorado Procurement Manual*[1] to be helpful. You can search for similar documents for your state.

Since I moved to Colorado, I have actually had more luck landing contracts with city and county governments than I have had with the state of Colorado. I have connected with clients through referrals and networking. A colleague sent me an RFP for training classes in Adams County, Colorado. The RFP process took awhile, but I was awarded a nice contract that has been renewed four years in a row (with another RFP in year 3). The entire process was no more difficult or cumbersome than the RFP process has been for my corporate clients, and the employees are delightful to teach.

You can also Google a local, county, or city government to find potential contacts in a target department. Then you can contact them just as you would contact corporate clients (by phone, mail, or e-mail), and with any luck they will tell you how to apply for contracts directly or through RFP.

---

[1] http://www.colorado.gov/dpa/dfp/sco/contracts/Contracts/Procurement_Manual.pdf

Another useful resource is the ReferenceUSA* database, the world's largest business database, available free or for a minimal charge in many local libraries. Find a library near you where you can access ReferenceUSA.[2] I am grateful for such easy and free access to market research.

You might also be able to find contracting opportunities through vendor fairs and assistance to minority vendors (women and certain ethnic groups) to work with local government entities (these opportunities rarely happen in corporations). Vendor fairs are often advertised in the newspaper or at Chamber of Commerce functions. When I lived in Minnesota, I was on a list to receive notifications of vendor fairs from the state of Minnesota and the Minnesota District Small Business Administration. You might call the appropriate agency within your state or local government to see if such fairs are scheduled.

Marketing to state and local governments

Now, look more deeply into mining your business research database. It will provide addresses, phone numbers, number of employees, and contact names (this last information must be verified, of course). If you are not certain whom to contact, you can call the main receptionist and ask for a contact name. Here is my script: "Hello! I need the name of the person who organizes training in your [city/county/agency]."

Notice, once again I used the verb *need* rather than *want*. And here's another distinction between corporate and government prospects: Most corporate receptionists will provide the name I need, but I've had a few say, "I'm sorry, I cannot give that information to the public." No worries: Government contact information is almost always public. Once I have a contact name, I launch a marketing campaign that might include a phone call, followed by mailings and follow-up phone calls. The goal is to arrange a meeting. (To learn more about cold calls like these, see Chapter 5, *Prospecting for Your Perfect Customer.*)

You might consider offering a free sample of your services as a part of your marketing plan. A contact at one state department asked me to donate my

---

[2] http://referenceusa.com/Static/LibraryLocator

expertise to a departmental Development Day, so I presented a free "Lunch 'n Learn" to 30 human resource directors in state agencies. It was a quick way to reach 30 potential contacts, and I landed a nice contract as a result.

The next time you think of your local or state government, analyze how you can help this market segment and build your bottom line at the same time. Government contracts can form a stable part of your portfolio.

CHAPTER 11

Could You, Should You, Move Your Business?

This chapter will share the processes and decisions I followed to move my business cross-country in 75 days. Some of my suggestions may help those who are firmly convinced, as I had been, that I could not relocate my business. Some of my ideas may help those who want to launch their independent careers (much of the relocation process is similar to launching a new business).

As I held him in my arms, I thought desperately, "I can't leave you! Although we just met, I know we'll have a perfect life together! I love you so much!"

But how could we make this relationship work at a distance of 900 miles? To be so far apart would be wrenching, but how could I leave behind my stable consulting and training business to relocate to another city? It seemed impossible.

I stared into his eyes. I just had to make this happen!

And then the pediatric nurse took my newborn grandson out of my arms and carried him off to the nursery, and although I had never before seriously considered moving my business from Minnesota to Colorado, I immediately kicked into gear.

Plan ahead

Once I had committed to moving to Colorado, my long-term goal was to complete the move within 12 to 18 months of Axel's birth. I thought that during that time, I would work very hard and get six months' living expenses in the bank to help finance my move.

However, on my next trip to Boulder to see my grandson, who was then five months old, I inadvertently bought a condo with a great room for my office. OK, it wasn't inadvertent, but it was rather sudden and made my adult children scratch their heads in surprise: I am usually methodical, even plodding, in my decision-making. I contracted to buy my new Colorado home within two days, sold my Minnesota house in five days, downsized 50 percent of my (pack rat) possessions, and started packing. I did plan ahead; I just planned and moved FAST.

While my move went pretty well, I would heartily recommend at least a year of planning a long-distance move, with several trips to your new location to scout for clients and potential business. Of course, there's always the feeling in an endeavor this huge that you would like just "one more day," but if you need to downsize at all, time is an asset.

I would also recommend that you set aside time right before your actual move and temporarily shut down your business. I taught four days a week until the day of my actual move, and even on that day, I taught a half-day, then drove my rented moving truck out of Minnesota into the sunset. It was insane (although the extra income provided a nice cushion to allow me some time to settle in Colorado). And if you can move in the spring or summer, you may find it easier to find your way around your new location than in the winter. My moving in November (just before the holidays) meant that I had to work around snow and the fact that no one had time to network with me right away.

Decide what to do with your business in your old location

I first considered selling my business to another entrepreneur in the Twin Cities. I teach technical and business writing in corporations. I had several local competitors, and I explored the concept of selling my accounts to them. However, after much discussion with other business owners, I realized that my independent business is not like a brick-and-mortar operation that can be sold turnkey. My relationships with my clients are so highly personalized that it would be hard to realize the full value of my business in an outright sale.

So I followed the path of another independent who had (coincidentally) moved to Denver two years earlier: I decided to commute back to the Twin

Cities one week a month to teach for my best accounts, at least until I became established in Colorado. After reading *Attracting Perfect Customers*[8], I had fairly well weeded out my less-than-perfect clients and had focused my energies on my best accounts.

I discussed my impending move with each important client and offered them my list of available dates in the following year. The universal response was congratulatory and celebratory, followed by discussions of how we could make the transition work for everyone.

Before I moved, I posted an article on my website explaining my move and stating that I would now be serving both Minnesota and Colorado businesses. Potential clients in Minnesota didn't seem to mind that I'd be flying in to teach their people. (I wonder if they viewed me as more of an expert because I came from another state?) It's hard to believe, but once I left the Twin Cities, I seemed to be in more demand than I had been before I moved. I even found three promising new accounts in the Twin Cities within three months of moving to Colorado.

If you are able to work at a distance, it might be advantageous to consider retaining your best clients in your former market, at least temporarily. For me, this meant traveling once a month because I deliver stand-up training, but the security of having a steady income while I looked for business in Colorado was well worth it. Depending on your circumstances, you may be able to pull off your transition without traveling as much.

I didn't raise my rates on my existing clients, even though I was incurring monthly travel costs; I simply absorbed these costs and viewed them as an incentive to search for business in my new city and state. To serve my Minnesota customers, I arranged for a toll-free number. Alas, none of them used this feature, so I cancelled the line.

Build your business in your new location

Marketing yourself in your new location is not all that different than marketing a newly launched independent business (except, perhaps, that you will have many years of experience and customer references from your prior location[s]).

I needed to employ all my prospecting and a marketing skills in Colorado. I went to the library and researched companies that might need my services (see Chapter 5, *Prospecting for Your Perfect Customer*). I wrote a new business plan and marketing plan for Colorado. And I started networking, as I describe in Chapter 21, *Networking for Independents*. My first experience was the Society for Technical Communication (STC) Rocky Mountain Chapter[1] meeting, where I passed out business cards, collected business cards, and wrote thank-yous for speaking with me. I volunteered to help my new STC community, which provided valuable visibility.

If you have more time than I did to plan your move, you can do a lot of this research at a distance; many local libraries have an online database of companies that you can search by size, industry, and location (or all of the above). You might subscribe to business magazines in your target area and use them to start building your own database of companies to target. And a few trips to meet with potential clients in your new city before you move might help your transition to your new market.

I also located Colorado's Business Resource Guide (free at the library) to help me understand what I needed to do to get my business registered with the Secretary of State.

Benefits of moving your business

Of course, moving for love is a positive experience, and I have not had one second thought or regret. I have witnessed Axel crawl for the first time, experienced his first bout with flu, and met his new sister two years later. Now I'm a "soccer Grandma" and I love all of it.

Your reason for moving may not be as exciting as love at first sight; perhaps you are moving because of an economic downturn in your area. Whatever prompts your move, your attitude will drive your results. I worked hard to reframe every complication in the moving process as just a necessary issue

---

[1] http://stcrmc.org/

to get through so that I could achieve my goal of spending more time with Axel. I banished the word "hassle" from my vocabulary as I tried to focus on the great benefits of the move.

Surprise! There were great benefits of the move:

Less stuff!

Purging my office of outdated files, equipment, and furniture brought great clarity and a sense of accomplishment. I moved only what was necessary, and I haven't missed a thing I discarded. My great discovery during this process was Craigslist.com, a free bulletin board on which you can post your possessions for sale in your local area. I sold over 35 items this way, including 3 desks, 5 filing cabinets, and other office equipment that I chose not to move. I learned to have faith that the right person would come along at the right time and buy my stuff at the right price (see Chapter 13, *The Zen of Craigslist*). It worked, both in Minnesota and Colorado, where I needed Craigslist to replace some equipment and furniture. My new, leaner office is easier to work in.

Exhilarating terror!

I had become complacent after 15 years in business in Minnesota, rarely trying something new. In my new environment, I tried to overcome my fears by going one new place each day and trying to target one new potential client each day. This method has worked to provide wonderful new clients here in Colorado to supplement my Minnesota clients. And I'm convinced that I would not have made all the changes I have made if I were still in my old, comfortable environment.

New clarity!

I became really clear about clients that I needed to keep in Minnesota and even more clear about what I wanted to "sell" to new clients in Colorado. I turned down a contract that didn't fit my strategic goals in Minnesota, and surprise!—two new contracts showed up within days that more than replaced the income I would have seen with the non-strategic contract.

On April 3, 2005, moving my business seemed impossible. On April 4, 2005 at 6:20 pm, when Axel was born, moving my business became both possible and absolutely necessary. Now, I wonder why I waited so long to make the move. I also wonder: If I achieved the impossible (to move my business), what else do I think is impossible but is actually achievable?

CHAPTER 12
The Goal Is to Get It Right, Not Be Right (Admitting Mistakes)

When you are an employee, you are evaluated and reviewed by management regularly, and you are probably also told when you make mistakes. Independents, on the other hand, may have to recognize their own mistakes—and that means developing self-awareness and fighting denial. I pretty much count on making at least one mistake a day, maybe more on Mondays and Fridays, which reduces the pressure of perfectionism and relieves the negativity of regret.

My accountant told me a funny story recently: Her toddler thinks that if he closes his eyes when playing "Hide and Seek," he becomes invisible. I immediately identified my own tendency toward ignoring or even denying when I have made a mistake or have failed at something.

Later that same day, I read an article in *The Economist* on "Womenomics" ("Feminist Management Theorists Are Flirting With Some Dangerous Arguments"[5]) that highlighted Dong Mingzhu, the boss of Gree Electric Appliances, an air-conditioning giant. She claims that she never admits her mistakes because she is always correct. Well, her company may have boosted shareholder returns by nearly 500 percent, but I hope that I am never known for boasting of my own perfection.

Mistakes vs failure

That is why I try hard to consciously reflect on my mistakes and failures so that I can get it right the next time. Wiktionary defines a *mistake* as an error or blunder.[1] For example, I recently mixed up invoices for two clients, both named Nancy. I undercharged one Nancy and overcharged the other Nancy. When I discovered my mistake, I immediately contacted the Nancy whom I had overcharged, apologized, and offered to reduce my next bill

---

[1] http://en.wiktionary.org/wiki/mistake

to her by the amount of the overage rather than have to figure out how to refund the money and get it into her system. Lesson learned: Slow down when invoicing!

A *failure*, by contrast, is defined as "not meeting a desirable or intended objective; opposite of success."[2] This definition implies that there are pre-established goals or standards (for example, performance appraisals, test scores, or deadlines). I experienced a painful failure in 2009 when I sat for the Board of Editors in the Life Sciences (BELS) examination (an editing test to become board-certified for editing in the life sciences)—and missed passing it by a few percentage points. I was chagrined and my ego was bruised, but I immediately dug in to study more math and statistics and passed the exam in 2010. A healthy dose of humility inspired me.

Business owners make—and can learn from—mistakes, too

Business owners often make mistakes and failures in at least two categories: those that affect others (for example, clients, vendors, students, other freelancers) and those that affect our business practices (for example, spending too much on phone service or not updating technical skills).

Here is what being in business since 1990 has taught me about my own mistakes and failures:

- The best plan is to immediately admit to others what my part was and ask: "How can I make this right?" Then I complete the amends or correction(s) promptly and cheerfully; I try not to apologize too much.
- To recognize mistakes that affect my business, I perform regular audits on operations, expenses, marketing, and my own educational needs. One such audit led me to switch to a pay-per-minute cell plan that (ironically) delivers better coverage for $40 less per month. Another self-audit brought the awareness that I was being charged $150 a year for my business credit card in return for miles for an airline that I never fly; I immediately changed credit cards and now receive money back

---

[2] http://en.wiktionary.org/wiki/failure

for every purchase (total savings: about $400 more a year). As an independent, I make many decisions every day while performing my work and running my business, and every decision could be a mistake or lead to failure. I am also the only one who can get it right.

- I used to have an innate fear of criticism, which I have tempered by participating in Toastmasters.[3] In the last eight years, I have given more than 90 speeches and benefited so much from immediate, constructive evaluations that I no longer cringe at criticism. Now, I even ask my clients for a retrospective after every project: What worked well, what didn't, how could I improve? Then I leverage the feedback into better performance.

- I'm trying to stop looking for others to blame. I am conscious when I'm projecting blame onto "the test," for example, or the designer on a project. I know that whenever I point my finger at someone or something else, there are three fingers pointing back at me.

- When I can't figure out my own pattern of mistakes or failures, I need to ask for help from fellow independents, friends, family, or a therapist. Sometimes my pattern is caused by deeply rooted emotional issues and I may need help to discern the pattern and its causes. Nothing changes if nothing changes, and nothing in my life will ever change unless I make the change within myself.

- I have learned that I cannot do the same thing over and over again and expect different results. I am responsible for "getting it right, not being right."

And, finally, I give thanks to all the 12-step recovery meetings that have taught me everything I know about mistakes, failures, amends, and progress—not perfection.

---

[3] http://www.toastmasters.org

CHAPTER 13

The Zen of Craigslist

Craigslist? Really? In a book about owning and operating your own independent business? You bet.

I am a great fan of free bulletin boards like Craigslist.[1] Craigslist allows individuals to post free ads in their local area. In the process of moving my business 900 miles from the Twin Cities west to Colorado in 2005, I sold more than 40 items (including desks, filing cabinets, and office equipment) on Craigslist and purchased about 15 items, including a new desk, for my new home and home office in Colorado.

I love the fact that Craigslist has always helped me sell my possessions for more than I could have received at a garage sale. I also love that I can purchase things that I want at 30% of retail. However, the real value of this experience has been what I have learned about writing, business, and myself in the process.

Lessons of Craigslist

Craigslist allows anyone to post an ad free (there are lots of categories, including employment, but in this chapter I'm writing only about selling and buying my household and office items). The site offers a simple process to digitally list and describe what you are selling, including setting a price and giving your general location to help buyers screen their searches.

Think about the details that are important to your buyer

Although there is apparently no limit on the amount of advertising text that one is allowed, I started off writing ads with minimal text and learned my first lesson: The buyer will let you know what you've left out, and the buyer is always right. I thought the most important details about my oak desk were its dimensions, but potential buyers e-mailed questions about the composition (oak veneer over pressboard); its age (less than five years);

---

[1] http://www.craigslist.com/

and the brand (Bell). Their queries provided a good lesson in marketing myself and my business: Do I really know what my potential clients want or need to know about my services? Am I leaving out details in my marketing materials that are important to them? I need to ask these questions and listen to their answers.

Create attractive photos and ad copy

My second lesson came as I learned to provide good pictures to post with each listing. At first, I thought it was enough to shoot one quick picture of the item on the garage floor. When I got better with "staging" the pictures by covering that old stained floor with sheets or shooting pictures at different angles and various lighting, I received more hits on my postings. Note to self: Be explicit, and creative, with my marketing graphics. Creating attractive word or digital pictures will help sell my business product, too (which is actually me).

Pricing is a strategy

My third lesson came in pricing my household goods for sale. I did my competitive shopping online, but in the beginning, I was hoping for more money for my desk or end table. I guess I was still attached to these possessions. After a listing languished for several days with no hits, I was forced to think about lowering the price.

Here's a practical hint: Craigslist provides an easy editing function, but don't just change the price on the original listing. Since listings are chronologically organized, your old listing may be 75 to 300 listings deep in the queue. Instead, copy the text of your old ad and delete the listing, then post a new listing with the lower price (you'll have to add the pictures again).

As for setting prices, used goods sell on Craigslist for between 30% and 50% of retail. Furniture such as desks or couches often sells at the lower end, but specialized items like IKEA® furniture or in-demand baby items like Britax® car seats will command 50% or more of their original price.

Pricing used goods for sale is, of course, different than pricing my services. However, the methods and principles are the same:

1. Research the competition
2. Price realistically
3. Be flexible when necessary

And don't take the market personally. Often, the rate we can command at any given time is affected by forces beyond our control.

Focus on small chunks at a time

My fourth lesson from Craigslist was to focus, focus, focus. At first I listed about ten items for sale concurrently, and I found myself totally distracted by the traffic. With the resulting flood of e-mail, I couldn't keep track of my inventory and potential buyers. Once I learned to post only a few items at a time, I found the process more manageable. This lesson reinforced what I know is true: I am more efficient if I focus fully on one task at a time.

Cross-sell when possible

After awhile, I realized I was cross-selling. The fellow who bought my bike rack mentioned canoeing, and I said I'd be selling my beloved canoe in a month. We negotiated a price and I called him when I was ready to part with it. I didn't even have to advertise. That experience led me to lesson number five: Always cross-sell my services. ("You don't need a class in technical writing? How about a class in creating better presentation slides?")

Patience is (still) a virtue

My final lesson was about patience. My first Craigslist posting, an oak secretary desk, sold in five hours. Wow, I thought, this will go fast! Then my next item, my high-tech canoe rack, didn't sell, although I received many inquiries. I let the ad run and moved on to list other things. A month later, I received a panicked e-mail; the buyer needed this rack immediately! Thirty minutes later, he drove off, smiling, with my canoe rack, and I had a fistful of cash and an important lesson about patience.

Life, the Universe, and Craigslist

But Craigslist taught me a much more profound truth about patience and the Universe. So far, this experience had served as a metaphor for my business practice, but the true message was much more metaphysical.

Craigslist taught me to trust in a universal principle: Everything sells to the right person at the right time at the right price: I was not in control of any of these variables. All I was responsible for was the footwork: Write the best, most explicit, most attractive marketing language that I could; set the fairest price I could determine; and then believe that the right person would come along and buy at the right time and price.

So I stopped fretting and started watching. Sure enough, a gentle, spiritual man bought my canoe, which had allowed me to access the wilderness of the Boundary Waters—a profoundly spiritual experience for me. An English teacher bought my favorite oak desk. A young couple with an energetic dog bought the huge doghouse that had housed my once-energetic dog.

Everyone I dealt with was respectful in negotiations and thrilled with their purchases. They smiled as they drove away and I smiled as I drove to the bank. I was grateful that worthy people were enjoying the things I no longer needed. Everything was happening as it should.

And of course, this is the message of *Attracting Perfect Customers*[8]. I've mentioned this book in other chapters, and I see the authors' message helping again in this chapter: "Expect your every need to be met, expect the answer to every problem, expect abundance on every level...."

Enlightenment

I do not fret as much about my income and my work much today. I trust that the Universe, or the God of my understanding, or something that I cannot even understand will deliver all three parts of the equation—although not necessarily at my price or timing.

I use this principle all the time in my business now. I am currently awaiting the results of a very large bid. The client is two weeks behind in the decision-making process, and I am amazingly calm. If the work comes to me, it was the right client at the right price and the right time. If not, the right client will come along at the right time and the right price. This belief frees a lot of energy to be plowed into my existing contracts, to provide the best service to my clients, to do my absolute best work for everyone, to market diligently, and to trust that the equation will work on my behalf. (Trusting a metaphysical equation is pretty ironic for an English major who avoids numbers.)

And the process does work. In the last 12 months, I have netted more income than ever before while worrying less. I've also had the most fun of my life with each contract. I'm grateful to Craigslist for helping me sell and buy household and office items, but, most importantly, for teaching me this valuable lesson.

5 quick business lessons learned from Craigslist

1. The user (buyer) is always right.
2. Use persuasive pictures to sell yourself.
3. When pricing yourself, research your competition; price realistically; be flexible when necessary.
4. Focus, focus, focus on one task at a time.
5. Be patient. Life doesn't usually happen on your time schedule.

CHAPTER 14

Reframing to Save our Sanity

Bad things do happen to good independents. If you are like me, I have always had a hard time shrugging off negative events; instead, I "grind" on things in the past that I cannot change. Perhaps my bid was rejected or a client just stopped returning phone calls or e-mails. Of course, worrying about the past drains my energy to deal with the present and affects my performance in my business. Learning to reframe negative events can save independents time and energy.

I recently had to reframe a bad personal experience in order to stop obsessing about it. My dog's right eye had to be removed because of a fast-growing tumor. The tumor turned out to be cancer, but fortunately it had not metastasized to her lymph nodes. The surgery was flawless and Emma adapted quickly (although she still bonks into me or others on her right side when running wildly in the dog park).

I emphasize her quick adaptation because I myself was not handling this drastic change in our lives well. I was still stuck in self-talk: "I had to take my dog to Englewood to have her eye removed. Why did this have to happen to us? Was there something that I was feeding her that caused the cancer? Were there alternatives to this surgery that we didn't consider? How will I ever be able to take her hiking in the mountains?" This negative thought process was certainly dragging me down.

And then, one sunny afternoon at our dog park, Emma and I met a small boy about three years old. Emma, who loves children, made friends with him right away. After a bit, the boy turned to me and said, rather profoundly, "Your pet has one eye," and went off to join his grandmother.

"That's it!" I said. "A three-year-old has enlightened me! Emma has one eye. I'm over it. We're moving ahead."

This stunning and sudden cognitive reframing of a painful situation brought me such serenity that I asked a few friends if they, too, had experienced positive reframing in their personal or professional life. Sarah, a personal trainer, told me of two clients, both of whom had broken bones in their feet from too much running. One client worked out on a spinning bike while healing and discovered that she loved spinning. Sarah's other client began swimming with great success. Another friend, Kit, told me of a sign in her company's customer service call center: "Your customer can hear the smile on your face." Kit said that she often thinks of that sign when speaking on the phone now, even when she's not feeling particularly smiley, so that she can reframe her day.

Others have pointed out the obvious negative forms of reframing that are so evident during election cycles ("death panels" and "47%" come to mind). Manipulative people everywhere reframe their points to gain advantage in an argument or negotiation. When reframing becomes spin, most people can recognize the manipulation.

But that's not the kind of reframing that can help us stop fighting reality and get back on track. Recently, I had a negative thought that rose out of nowhere to threaten my sanity: I started resenting how small my office is, how hard it is to keep stuff from piling up. Yet it was I who chose to purchase this small condo so I could live in a very expensive town near my grandchildren—and nothing had changed in my finances so that I could now afford to buy a big house instead. I set out to reframe my perceptions:

1. I did have a BIG office back in Minnesota and it was even more cluttered than my office is now.
2. My current office, while small, is well laid out and functions well.
3. This office has six hours of southern sun a day, but my Minnesota office faced north and never received a moment's sun.
4. I am fundamentally opposed to collecting too much stuff, and this small office discourages collecting stuff.

SO, THIS OFFICE IS JUST RIGHT FOR ME RIGHT NOW.

I filed a pile of stuff; the office looked bigger; and I moved into acceptance. Next step, serenity and sanity!

I always suspect that people who work in corporations or organizations have colleagues around them to help them reframe painful or negative events or situations, while independent freelancers are totally isolated. Neither position is probably absolutely true. Let's reframe that perception that freelancers are isolated: We don't have to be isolated. We can establish a circle of trusted advisors who steer us toward productive reframing; we don't have to feel alone. (See Chapter 17, *The Power of Groups to Support the Freelancer*, to learn more about the benefits of supporting and being supported by groups.)

So if you are dwelling on something negative that has happened to you, I encourage you to find someone to help you reframe your pain. A project was cancelled: Your friend-advisor may point out that you were having a hard time working with the client on this project. He or she might suggest that now you can use your time to market your business to companies closer to your office.

Of course, as you might expect, there is an Internet tool called the Reframing Matrix[1] that can help business teams—and perhaps you, too—develop reframing skills.

---

[1] http://www.mindtools.com/pages/article/newCT_05.htm

CHAPTER 15

The Power of Certification for Independents

Some freelancers who seek a marketing advantage may earn certification to prove their skills. This path can be expensive and time-consuming, but it can also be financially and personally rewarding.

A former student e-mailed that she had enrolled in a certification course after a year of unemployment. I congratulated her but wondered privately why it had her taken so long to take this action after losing her job. Was it fear, or cost, or the sense that she knew enough already?

Perhaps I see value in certification because I am an official "Learner," according to my StrengthsFinder 2.0[1] assessment: "You love to learn...you will always be drawn to the process of learning. The process, more than the content or the result, is especially exciting for you."

With a graduate degree that is 25 years old, I know that I must constantly renew my learning to demonstrate competency and proficiency. I love learning at professional conferences, but just attending sessions can be eclectic, unstructured, and rarely documented. Therefore, I have recently sought certification in medical editing to add to my services as a corporate trainer in medical manufacturing firms. For me, training and medical editing enhance each other and provide balance, variety, and relative security in a risky economy.

I have mentioned before that to gain credibility for my editing services I joined AMWA (American Medical Writers Association)[2] and enrolled in their Essential Skills certification process (eight courses), which I completed in 2010—and immediately enrolled in the next certificate program, to be awarded in 2013. I also sat for the BELS examination (Board of Editors in

---

[1] http://www.strengthsfinder.com/home.aspx
[2] http://www.amwa.org/

the Life Sciences)[3] and passed the exam in 2010. Both processes are rigorous, requiring extensive study and humbling tests on subjects like statistics and numbers, which I, an English major, have carefully avoided throughout my career.

What professional certification opportunities are out there?

There are at least three formats used as a basis for professional certification: examination, course completion, or portfolio review.

The Society for Technical Communication (STC) offers online certificate course[4] in such areas as "Writing Effective User Documentation," "Tech-Comm101," and "Usability Testing Essentials: Hands-on Workshop and Best Practices."

STC also offers a portfolio-based Certified Professional Technical Communicator™ (CPTC) credential[5] for six core competency areas of practice (user analysis, document design, project management, authoring, delivery, and quality assurance). According to Steven Jong, chair of the certification committee implementing STC certification, "Certification raises professional standards, increases respect, and reduces employers' risk in hiring decisions, since hiring the wrong person can cost a great deal. Employers compete for certified professionals, which drives the salary gap between certified and non-certified professionals. Depending on the profession, that difference in salary may be up to 30%." (A 2007 AMWA survey found significant increases of up to 25% for respondents with AMWA certificates.)

Jong expects the largest single block of applicants for STC certification to be independent technical communicators and lone writers, so his committee is working to make sure that their portfolios are assessed accurately and treated equally to communicators in large, supportive environments. "The challenge is to assess the applicant and not the environment," says Jong.

---

[3] http://bels.org
[4] http://www.stc.org/education/online-education/certificate-courses?view=category
[5] http://www.stc.org/certification

STC member Tammy Van Boening, owner of Spectrum Writing,[6] praises her certification in Instructional System Design: "It helped me land a 15-month contract when a potential client wanted to know if I could turn participant guides and facilitator guides into training for them."

Rich Maggiani, President of Solari Communication[7] and an STC Fellow, is looking forward to becoming certified: "Certification has become the de facto standard for other professional organizations and is becoming one also for the IABC (International Association of Business Communicators).[8] I expect that, over time, the same will occur for technical communication certification."

As for me, I believe certification has enhanced my credibility and marketability. Of course, the process has been and continues to be expensive. My investment in my two AMWA certificates alone is at least $1,800 out of pocket plus more than 80 hours of study per certificate. However, my income has steadily increased along with the quality of the projects that I have been awarded.

That is why I agree with Derek Bok, former president of Harvard: "If you think education is expensive, try ignorance."

---

[6] http://www.spectrumwritingllc.com/home/

[7] http://solari.net/

[8] http://www.iabc.com/

CHAPTER 16
Are You a Craftsperson or an Entrepreneur?

At some point in your freelance career, you may need to decide whether to remain a craftsperson practicing work that you love or to strike out as an entrepreneur, making money through your business skills rather than through performing the actual service your company provides. Either path is fine, but you will have more peace if your direction is intentional and not accidental.

I hate when this happens: My son, to whom I have vowed never to deliver unsolicited advice, calls me and says, "Mom…Mom…I want you to read the greatest business book. It will help your business so much!"

"Sure, sure," I say, to buy time. I'm thinking that I have no intention of ordering this book, since my son has been an employee—a commercial pilot—his entire career. He is, though, an entrepreneur wannabe and has great ideas (a teahouse in Anchorage; an aviation-themed coffee shop chain) that he hasn't yet been able to act upon.

"No, really, Mom. You and I have talked about selling your business in the next seven years. This book will help you reach that goal!"

And even then I have no desire to read the book. But a funny thing happened the next day: My business coach suggested that I read the very same book for the very same reasons and more.

So I broke down and ordered *The E-Myth Revisited*[7] by Michael E. Gerber. As I read, I kept finding things I didn't agree with, rather than looking for what I could gain from the book. But that soon changed, and I felt a shift in my business thinking and practice. In this chapter, I'll share what Gerber taught me about managing my business.

Three roles

Gerber defines the E-Myth as the myth of the entrepreneur: that you and I, as entrepreneurs, can do it all—can be entrepreneur, manager, and technician (craftsperson) in our own businesses. He says that these three personalities are always struggling for power within us, and until we can free our entrepreneur from managerial and technician roles, we will not succeed as entrepreneurs. (This was where I first balked at Gerber's message, but I read on.)

Gerber describes an entrepreneur, Sarah, who learned from her aunt to bake fabulous pies and opened a pie shop in honor of that aunt. When we meet her, she's doing it all: mopping the floor, purchasing the flour, baking the pies, working incredible hours. Throughout the rest of the book, Gerber gently leads Sarah to understand that she cannot continue this way without burning out, and he shows her a vision of a better way.

Sarah learns that her passion for pies is good; a great entrepreneur will be, first, a craftsperson who knows what a "genuine fascination for truly astonishing little things done exactly right can have on the world" (p. xv). She learns to re-create her business using an organizational chart with at least 11 positions. She writes a position contract and summarizes the results to be achieved by each position. Then she signs the contract for each role.

Why do that? Because Sarah (and you and I, if we choose) must prototype the position in order to replace ourselves with a system. This was the point where I stopped resisting Gerber's book and method. I realized that, without a system in my company, I was just doing tactical work, not strategic work.

Take my bookkeeping, for example. I recently had a very profitable year. Because I had worked so much to earn that profit, I was way too busy to do my bookkeeping (after all these years in business, I was still keeping my own books, a job I truly hate). So I waited and waited until I could find time to do my books—until my accountant said, "Produce the numbers or I can't help you with your taxes." It was a scramble, but I met his deadline. I could have reduced my level of stress and saved time, energy, and money by hiring a bookkeeper much earlier in the year!

Franchise or not?

And so, following Gerber's suggestions, I interviewed bookkeepers. Because I was raised in a self-sufficient home where my mother sewed all our clothes and cooked every meal we ate, this idea of not doing my own books was foreign to me. But it is clear that I can't be visionary when I'm wallowing in numbers (which I hate). My bookkeeper not only gave me more time to run my business, but she helped me view my business finances more clearly and strategically than I can when I'm drowning in the numbers myself.

Just knowing that I'm going to be freed of a job I hate always gives me energy to start visualizing my business direction as Gerber directs. He touts the franchise model, where every detail of the business can be recreated identically to provide a turnkey business opportunity, systematized and applied intentionally by another businessperson. (I rejected this concept at first, until I read that Gerber suggests proceeding with the franchise model until the entrepreneur has documented every possible procedure and detail. Then the business will run much better even if the entrepreneur never takes it to franchise.)

As Gerber says, "systematizing your business need not be a dehumanizing experience, but quite the opposite!" (p. 210). He describes the Venetian Hotel in Capitola, California, whose owner systematized both his vision and every detail of that vision in order to deliver an amazing night's rest and more to every patron, consistently, time after time. For this business owner, the system was the solution.

So, surprise! I now document every process in my business, including the dreaded bookkeeping/finance process. (I use FreeMind[1], a shareware mind-mapping program, to create a mind map on the fly; then I formalize the procedure later.)

But, still, a franchise?

And then a member of my extended family sat me down at our recent reunion and asked me if I'd consider franchising my teaching business. He

---

[1] http://freemind.sourceforge.net/wiki/index.php/Main_Page

wanted to deliver training in Bend, Oregon, and had no idea how to go about it. Hmmm…an interesting synchronicity. I thought about the three people in Minnesota who had approached me to buy my business there after I moved to Colorado. Maybe the franchise idea isn't so wild, after all.

I have since decided to generate more income by monetizing my training content—licensing my intellectual property to corporations for their trainers to use. This is a better model for me than franchising, but I am grateful that I didn't reject the franchise idea because it eventually led to this decision. Gerber helped me change my mind, and my new endeavor is proving to be very profitable.

Passion and commitment

And that's why I think freelancers should read Gerber's book. I've read all these ideas before, but I've never encountered them so humanly explained and illustrated. It's the first time I've seen "good business practices" linked with passion and commitment to my vision. All the examples Gerber provides have convinced me that I can rethink my business, even after being solo since 1990, and I can take it in some visionary directions, just as my son urged.

Got any more good books to recommend, Bruce?

CHAPTER 17

The Power of Groups to Support the Freelancer

The working style of solo practitioners such as writers, editors, graphic designers, desktop publishers, and photographers is often a paradox. By choosing to remain self-employed rather than seek employment in a company, we demonstrate our need and desire for autonomy. However, we still need and probably crave interaction with others; therefore, many of us seek out groups, both existing and self-formed, for networking, interaction, and support.

Employees are surrounded by an involuntary community, but the freelancers I know have an almost "no-one-is-an-island" need for community, and that fascinates me. I read in *The Economist* that sports training in a group may heighten an individual's tolerance for pain and allow him or her to train longer and harder ("Fitter with friends"[6]). Biologists think that the positive effects of community may be part of an evolved mechanism that rewards group interaction with endogenous opioids (endorphins), or a legal high. Sounds great to me!

In this chapter, I will explore the range of communities that independents may belong to on a continuum from formal to informal (and sometimes ad hoc). I will relate what some Society for Technical Communication (STC) Consulting and Independent Contracting Special Interest Group (CIC SIG)[1] members shared in an informal survey conducted in early April 2010, attributing quotes where respondents provided their names. I will tell about my own involvement with group support and close the chapter with a few tips on improving your own behavior in the communities that you seek out.

---

[1] http://www.stcsig.org/cic/

Why freelancers belong to groups

Many freelancers are members of long-standing professional and formal organizations such as STC or the American Medical Writers Association (AMWA).[2] We seek technical answers, professional opportunities, business advice, networking, friendships, and fun from these groups. One respondent said: "Belonging to STC and attending local chapter meetings gave me the chance to network with other writers/editors, affirmed my belief that I was in a profession with other like-minded and very nice people, and provided inspiration to pursue my Masters in technical communication."

Another respondent had a similarly useful group experience: Kathleen McIlraith found the STC Instructional Design and Learning SIG (IDL SIG)[3] particularly useful "during these months when I've been unable to find employment as a Technical Writer or an Instructional Designer... [it] has provided lively discussion on issues and furnished me with additional reading so I stay current."

Likewise, Rhonda Bracey of CyberText Consulting[4] shares a positive experience with groups: "When I started in technical communication, I taught myself WinHelp. I had no one to turn to when I was stuck—I live in Western Australia where there are no support groups. I discovered the HATT (Help Authoring Tools and Techniques) discussion group[5] and received an enormous amount of help from the members, none of whom talked down to this 'newbie.' From HATT, I discovered STC and the Lone Writer[6] and CIC SIGs. All have helped me often. I couldn't be a lone writer without these support groups."

Another respondent said: "When I was moving from unstructured FrameMaker to structured FM as a lone writer, the FrameMaker forums and listservs were invaluable. Every question I had was thoughtfully answered, with examples...even to the point of viewing my own files and making suggestions."

[2] http://www.amwa.org/
[3] http://www.stcidlsig.org/wp/
[4] http://www.cybertext.com.au/
[5] http://groups.yahoo.com/group/HATT/
[6] http://www.stc-lonewriter.org

How to best work with your groups

But for many of us, professional groups fulfill only part of our need for engagement. In my personal life, I have turned to communities such as circuit training classes at my gym and several 12-Step recovery groups. It was through these experiences that I learned what the goal of belonging to a group should be: Give as much as you can to the group, and you'll reap much more than you sow. I have found lifelong friends in these groups, people I can help and can turn to for help.

Respondents also noted that small, personal groups could be very supportive. McIlraith cited a positive story about the power of community for personal growth or healing: "I facilitated a group of women in the 1990s who were diagnosed with either multiple sclerosis or fibromyalgia. Over 6 months of weekly meetings and discussions, each woman's disease went into remission as they encouraged and mentored one another."

Of course, not all communities are helpful. One respondent compared good group behavior ("No one in the group saw themselves better than anyone else. Everyone recognized that the total was much stronger than the individual parts") to a dysfunctional group in which the manager intentionally set up competition among group members and played favorites about who was the cream of her crop. I am sure you would agree: If possible, avoid interacting in a group like that one!

A group of two?

Sometimes, just one other person can help you as an independent, as Laura Ricci of 1Ricci[7] offers: "I was working onsite with a new client and was asked to solve a problem with software that I didn't have the best experience with, so I posted to the group and got some suggestions; one person was able to take a phone call with me to try to find a work-around."

---

[7] http://1ricci.com/

No group available? Form your own!

I am a true believer in groups, having formed my own informal communities when there did not appear to be an existing group that could meet my own needs. For example, in graduate school, I started a dissertation support group that provided accountability and an opportunity to get feedback on academic writing issues. Dissertation in hand, I started a job search support group that helped with job search strategy, resumes, and cover letters; we videotaped mock interviews and gave each other feedback. Once I had landed a job, I faced divorce and began a divorce support group to guide me through another rocky period. Another independent, a military wife on a small base in Texas, created an ad-hoc baby-sitting co-op.

A few tips about working with your groups

1. Approach a community with the idea of "How can I help others in the group?" rather than "How can I get my needs met?" You may have joined the group to meet your needs, but paradoxically, the more you give, the more you receive.

2. If you find any group too large and intimidating, join or form sub-groups. The STC CIC SIG discussion board is a great introduction to the larger society. If your professional organization seems overwhelmingly large, perhaps you could join a committee and get to know a few people who might then introduce you to others in the larger group. I practiced this principle when I moved into my condo in 2005; I was totally overwhelmed by the size of this development (448 units). Soon, however, I was elected to the Board of Directors, which brought me into contact with a 9-person subgroup. At our dog park, I found many new human and canine friends. I also joined our community garden and met other gardeners. Gradually, I found myself feeling less isolated in this huge property and now feel very lucky to be a resident of such a richly diverse, supportive community.

Still skeptical about groups? View *This Emotional Life*,[8] a PBS documentary in three parts hosted by Harvard psychologist and best-selling author Daniel

---

[8] http://www.pbs.org/thisemotionallife/

Gilbert. The documentary cites overwhelming evidence that points to one conclusion: Long-term happiness depends on the quality of your relationships. My own experience and this brief research have proven to me that groups provide freelancers with a great source of potential professional relationships and happiness.

Marketing

CHAPTER 18
Building a Marketing Plan

Just as most freelancers have had no formal training in business before we launch our businesses, most of us likewise have had no formal training in the business disciplines of marketing or selling. And many of us grew up hearing, "Don't brag about yourself." It is no wonder we need to learn to market and sell ourselves every day so we can grow our businesses.

When I was a single mom with young children, I usually served oatmeal for breakfast. My children objected bitterly, demanding more expensive cold cereal brands. I used these selling points to convince them: Oatmeal is cheap, fast, warm, and healthy. And I had to adapt each point to my audience, selling the benefits rather than features of oatmeal: "Saving money on breakfast means we'll have more money for your hockey equipment."

It must have worked. Before a backpacking trip to the Rockies years later, my 17-year-old son and I shopped for provisions. I was stunned when he grabbed a box of oatmeal packets at Safeway, and even more surprised when every morning, he left the tent early and cooked—oatmeal! When I asked him why, he responded with all the benefits I had tried to sell years earlier—with a few extra: Oatmeal is light in the backpack, doesn't get crushed like cold cereal, and doesn't need milk!

Selling did not come automatically to me. For my first few years in business, I operated under the mantra "If you build it, they will come." But the Field of Dreams approach doesn't usually work in real life; dedicated marketing is necessary to sell most services and products. Unfortunately, we may not know intuitively how to plan a marketing strategy, and we may feel uncomfortable selling ourselves and our services.

There are at least two reasons for this ignorance and reluctance. First, most academic institutions do not offer formal training in marketing and selling outside of business courses in their business schools. Second, many of us grew up being chided not to brag about our accomplishments. Humility, not self-promotion, was held up as a virtue.

So it's no wonder that when I launched my independent training business, I had fuzzy marketing and selling skills and an aversion to these activities. Finally, though, I got hungry enough to realize that I had to market and sell my services. First, I created a business plan. (For more information about business plans, read Chapter 3, *Business Plans Build Good Businesses*.) I wrote and implemented a marketing plan as a part of my business plan. And the best news was that I found many resources along the way and actually learned not to hate marketing!

Benefits of a marketing plan

Let's define marketing as a strategic collection of activities intended to support a company's image and increase sales. Marketing is a process, not an event. By contrast, advertising (direct mail, media ads, trade show presentations, and so on) is an event, a tactic you use to implement your marketing strategy. In this chapter, we'll focus on the strategic marketing plan and deal with tactical material in the next three chapters.

Your marketing plan, like your business plan, can be structured any way you want it. However, there are certain standard sections that might help you understand your business better:

1. Executive Summary
2. Target Markets
3. Marketing Plan Strategy
4. Expense Budget Summary
5. Sales Forecast
6. Measurement and Comparison
7. Marketing Organization
8. Critical Issues

To see what others have included in their marketing plans, visit the Resource List[1] (of course, a solo freelancer's marketing plan will look quite different than the plan for a skateboard shop). Then consider this powerful, brief exercise in marketing: the Seven-sentence Marketing Plan.

---

[1] http://www.textdoctor.com/bizresources/

The Seven-sentence Marketing Plan

This shortened marketing plan was first proposed by Jay Conrad Levinson, the creator of the Guerrilla Marketing[2] concept, now a branded marketing technique. In his book *GUERRILLA MARKETING: Secrets for Making Big Profits From Your Small Business*[9], first published in 1983 and republished in 2007, Levinson advocated revolutionary marketing tactics for small businesses as an alternative to expensive standard marketing efforts. The "guerrilla" metaphor plays on his insistence that entrepreneurs can adapt to market changes faster than larger companies can, thereby developing "weapons" appropriate to their specific businesses—and half of those weapons do not cost money (for example, niche/positioning, flexibility, sharing with others, enthusiasm, and credibility).

Levinson focuses on helping entrepreneurs who lack formal training in marketing, and the short plan is a good starting place for independent professionals just getting familiar with marketing. It's brief enough that you can generate your first draft in 10 to 15 minutes. I once led a small group in this exercise, and participants, including me, completed their drafts within 12 minutes; nevertheless, our finished products were comprehensive enough that we could use them to develop a detailed marketing plan section under each step.

Here are Levinson's seven steps:

1. Describe your identity.
2. State the purpose of your marketing.
3. Tell how this purpose will be achieved, focusing on the benefits of your offering.
4. Define your target audience.
5. Define your niche in the market.
6. Describe your proposed marketing vehicles.
7. Set your marketing budget as a percentage of projected gross sales.

---

[2] http://www.gmarketing.com/

You may be surprised by the designation of a marketing budget as a percentage of gross sales. That was an eye-opener for me! I had always thought of marketing expenses as discretionary, and when I was feeling pinched financially, I would eliminate spending on marketing. Once I had committed to spending a certain amount as an investment in future income, I began to market myself effectively and saw a substantial increase in my income.

I think what had confused me was the idea of "spending" as an investment, although I had no problem spending on a new computer as an investment! If you, too, have trouble spending for marketing, consider reading some of the books and websites listed in the Resource List[3] to learn how to invest your marketing money wisely.

Marketing: Translate features into benefits

Another good lesson I learned from the seven-sentence exercise was to translate features into benefits. Because I had never been trained in sales or marketing, it took me a while to figure out that people don't buy features (facts about a service or product); they buy benefits (especially benefits that solve a problem they are having). When my old computer kept crashing, I justified a new computer by focusing on the benefits of faster speed and more reliability. Finally, I realized that benefits solve problems.

Upon reflection, I realized that I had actually sold oatmeal to my children by promoting its benefits. One feature of oatmeal is that it is much cheaper than packaged cereal (and the benefit I had stressed was more money to spend on hockey equipment). Another feature of oatmeal is its high-fiber content (although I never was able to promote that as a benefit to my young children.) Other feature-to-benefit conversions were less tangible for my family (the fast-cooking feature was more of a benefit for me).

Recognizing that I had successfully practiced marketing skills in the past helped me when I went solo; I drew on those skills to start translating my features into benefits for my clients. My graduate degree was a feature, but it brought benefits to my clients: They knew I could finish extended writing

---

[3] http://www.textdoctor.com/bizresources/

projects and survive fierce editing cycles. My independent status was a benefit to them because they could hire me only when they needed me.

Value proposition

The next level of benefits statements is a value proposition, or a statement of the value that I will bring to the client. I learned a lot about this from Jill Konrath.[4] Jill says, "Powerful value propositions focus on the business outcomes companies get from using your products or services. Framed in business terminology, they highlight specific measurable results they address critical business issues AND demonstrate significant value." Read more about value propositions in Chapter 19, *Flex Your Marketing Muscles: Tactics for Reluctant Marketers.*

I had to train myself in marketing, and you can too. Read a few of the marketing books listed in the Resource List.[5] Then visit a few of the websites listed. Finally, approach three successful independents and ask them what marketing strategies work for them. These practical exercises are certainly not the equivalent of a Master's in marketing, but they may be all that you have time for.

If you asked me, the three marketing tips that I would give you include having a website. I would also mention my Constant Contact® newsletter that I send out monthly as a way to stay in touch with my readers, clients, and potential clients. Third: Engage in all the social media that you can. Finally, I would praise the visibility that results from my volunteer work for professional organizations such as the Society for Technical Communication (STC) and the American Medical Writers Association (AMWA) as a huge source of new business. (There: I gave you four tips. I always try to over-deliver.)

---

[4] http://www.jillkonrath.com/
[5] http://www.textdoctor.com/bizresources/

CHAPTER 19

Flex Your Marketing Muscles: Tactics for Reluctant Marketers

Few freelancers wake up in the morning eager to market themselves. But marketing is like swimming: If you stop, you sink. You might consider developing marketing tactics in three possible categories:

1. *High-tech*
2. *High-touch*
3. *High-credibility*

Read on to learn more about these three categories and find tips generously shared by many fellow freelance independents who responded to a survey asking them to share marketing tips.

I don't like to exercise. I particularly don't like to lift weights, but I like to have lifted weights. I can clearly see the benefits: muscle tone, strength, stress relief, weight management, a sense of satisfaction. In spite of these perceived benefits, I whine all the way to the gym. Afterwards, I am glad that I worked out.

Likewise, I don't like to market myself. Sometimes I think, "Heck [or stronger], I'm good at what I do. I've been doing this since 1990. People should seek me out!" Then I come to my senses, review my marketing plan, and get on with it. (To learn more about marketing plans, see Chapter 18, *Building a Marketing Plan*.)

The truth is: I don't like to market my services, but I like to have marketed my services. I like the income and security that comes after diligent marketing. Of course, you are right: Marketing is hard work! But so is starvation.

Developing tactics

Basically, your marketing plan is a document in which you spell out who you are, what you do, and what you don't do. You'll determine your target market and develop the benefits of your offering for that market. Most important, you will set your marketing budget as a percentage of your projected gross sales.

Next, you'll need to define tactics to accomplish your marketing goals. Start by reading Paul and Sarah Edwards and Jay Conrad Levinson (see the Resource List[1] for full information about some helpful resources).

Develop an "elevator speech" that briefly describes what you can do for a potential client—the rule of thumb states that the message should last no longer than an average elevator trip. Carol Elkins of A Written Word[2] has a ten-second reply to the question, "What do you do?" She has also developed a 30-second introduction that explains more about her business and the potential benefits of hiring her. Betsy Frick (no relation to me, but a good friend and former independent who has retired) shared this elevator speech: "I help people in business, government, and nonprofit agencies write things that others can read once and understand what to do."

Although we are small businesses, we can use big-business marketing tactics such as account penetration. Linda Gallagher of TechCom Plus, LLC,[3] calls this "garnering more work from existing clients." She cross-sells, looking for other client products she can help with. She may create documentation first, then offer to improve website content, marketing materials, training materials, product user guides, sales or training demos, or user interfaces for the same client. (See Chapter 7, *Telescoping for Survival*.)

Schedule your marketing. When you are in startup mode, you may be spending 100% of your time marketing. When you are more established as a business, you'll have to spend more time on billable hours and less time marketing. Just don't forget to schedule marketing time (perhaps set time for phoning or mailing on Friday afternoon or Monday morning when client deadlines may seem less demanding). The key is to schedule marketing time on your calendar.

---

[1] http://www.textdoctor.com/bizresources/
[2] http://www.awrittenword.com/
[3] http://techcomplus.com/

Consider developing marketing tactics in three possible categories: high-tech, high-touch, or high-credibility. It's best to have a mix of all three so that you can be sure to appeal to a wide variety of audiences.

High-tech marketing tactics

These strategies include a website, e-mail, TV, and social media. One excellent benefit of a website is that it can act as a high-tech brochure. When I started my business, I hired a designer for my website, but I have always maintained it myself. Today, WordPress makes it easier for freelancers to design and maintain their own websites. You may want to hire a content strategist to help with search engine optimization to improve your Google rating so that new customers can find you online more quickly.

Some independents use e-mail as a marketing tool. Consider sending an introductory e-mail to promote your services to small companies. You'll need to find the decision-maker who actually hires freelancers, not just someone in Human Resources. Learn more in Chapter 5, *Prospecting for Your Perfect Customer.*

Add a tagline to your e-mail signature and business card explaining your business, as Angela Wiens of Meridian Communications Inc.[4] does: "Technical Writing | Instructional Design | Information Design."

Most independents recognize that commercial TV ads are impossibly expensive for their budget, but media opportunities do exist. I once appeared on a friend's cable show (all cable stations must give free access to anyone who wants to have a show.) A viewer called the station, got my name, and hired me for a small project.

High-touch marketing tactics

If you view high-tech tactics as too cold and remote, high-touch tactics may allow you to feel more personal as you market the benefits you can bring to clients. High-touch tactics include networking, volunteering, mailing, phoning, and joining organizations.

---

[4] http://www.meridiancom.ca/

Networking is an effective high-touch tactic. Chapter meetings of professional organizations and associations are effective networking venues. For example, Wiens attends events hosted by Canadian Women in Communications (CWC).[5]

Rahel Bailie of Intentional Design Inc.[6] urges independents to "Get outside your peer-to-peer networking circles; you need to get in the faces of the decision-makers, whether it be at events for executives or [while] cold-calling…go to at least one meeting a week, even if you have a contract for the next six months." She suggests that you follow up with good networking etiquette. For example, send notes and offer resources to demonstrate your helpfulness.

Volunteering can provide a fertile source of leads. Years ago, I served on an STC committee (Society for Technical Communication),[7] where I met a fellow member who referred me to her training department. I landed a $10,000 contract! Another freelancer offered a free, drop-in consultation to small business members of her local Chamber of Commerce. She received free visibility and credibility that ultimately put her in contact with clients ready to buy.

Mailing can be economical and effective. Several independents mentioned "drip marketing," a strategy that calls for you to send prospective clients something through the mail or electronically on a regular basis. These pieces should provide information that will help educate the prospect and, occasionally, mention what you do.

---

[5] http://www.cwc-afc.com/
[6] http://intentionaldesign.ca/about-idi/
[7] http://stc.org

Here's an example offered by another colleague:

> My client's firm coached high-level investment brokers whose clients had liquid
> assets of $5M or more. I wrote a series of ten letters that were sent to pro-
> spective clients every month. The letters dealt with investment strategies for
> that particular audience. In the first letter, we said we were providing this
> education campaign and previewed what would come up. In letter 4, we invited
> them to a seminar, along with the education piece. In letter 7, we asked if we
> could call. In letter 10, we did so again. Each letter gave the recipient a chance
> to opt out of the series at any time by calling the office. At no time did the
> firm [cold] call the prospects—the prospects had to call the firm. This approach
> was very successful for this firm and with these potential clients. The letters
> were educational—a lot of research went into them—and it was a logically
> ordered way to present the information.

The concept of mailing also involves sending useful information to clients,
even when you are not currently working on a project with them. Mary Jo
David of Write Away Enterprises[8] says, "When I read an interesting article
on the Internet that I think would interest a particular client, I send the
link...with a quick note saying that the article is something I thought he/she
would be interested in and then add a 'hope business is good' kind of note.
I feel it's a way to put my name in front of the client without appearing
self-serving."

Phoning, especially cold calls, may be the least favorite marketing method
of most independents, but it can provide new leads and stir interest among
existing clients. Paula Foster hired a cold-calling coach who guided her
through the process of preparing for and making her first cold calls.

Levinson's *Guerilla Marketing*[9] will show you the benefits of writing a
script for your calls. According to Levinson, cold calling works far better
for businesses selling to other businesses than it does in direct consumer
selling. That may mean less rejection than in consumer telemarketing. Experienced marketers compute rejection as a part of their return on investment (for example, 10 hours of cold calling might result in 97 rejec-
tions—and 3 sales at $5,000 a sale.)

---

[8] http://www.writeawayent.com/

Join organizations to expand your network. This tactic works best if you also volunteer and network strategically within those organizations.

High-credibility marketing tactics

Consider publishing articles, competing for awards, getting elected to office in organizations, and offering presentations as ways to establish your credibility; potential clients will not feel they have to vet your qualifications before they hire you.

Publishing includes writing bylined articles. Sarah O'Keefe of Scriptorium[9] touts publishing as a long-term marketing strategy. She says that employees at her company "write books, publish white papers, and speak at conferences. These activities rarely cause immediate sales…but they result in leads months later. Over a period of years, our visibility pays off when people remember to call us for their projects. The key is to provide valuable information rather than a sales pitch."

Winning awards can build your credibility. Are you aware that many awards go begging for lack of applicants? Take a shot at an appropriate award. (As hockey icon Wayne Gretzky once pointed out, "You miss 100 percent of the shots you never take.") Think how nice that phrase "award-winning" will look on your marketing materials.

Getting elected to office is probably initially easier than winning awards, but you will have to do a lot of unpaid work. The good news is that your fellow volunteers can provide referrals and potential business contacts. I always hope that having served as president of both my STC and AMWA chapters will qualify me as credible in the eyes of potential clients.

Offering presentations can provide excellent leads. Consider teaching a continuing education class at your local community college. The pay is nominal, but participants may contact you later for personal coaching or to help with communication issues within their companies. I have hired several subcontractors on the basis of their impressive presentations.

---

[9] http://www.scriptorium.com/

I, too, have found that offering free seminars is a wonderful source of leads. I have a list of nonprofits to which I offer one seminar a year. Each free presentation takes about six hours of my time. As a return on my marketing investment, I often land training contracts from attendees. The key to success is to establish your criteria, design a speaker's packet, and send it to target organizations in the spring, when most new boards are trying to establish their programs for the fall and beyond.

But what about your stage fright? Get yourself to Toastmasters.[10] Even as an experienced public speaker, I still belong to Toastmasters to improve my self-confidence and speaking ability.

As you can see, all these tactics have worked to provide marketing muscle for independents, as well as visibility and credibility. Bailie suggests that you work these tactics in tandem. For example, combine speaking with networking, or do a phone campaign before (or after) a mail campaign.

Did someone say tandem? That reminds me: I DO like to bike, and I like to HAVE biked.

---

[10] http://www.toastmasters.org/

CHAPTER 20

Marketing 101: Learning from Other Independents

Successful independents know that marketing often involves annoying drudge work, expense, and salesmanship. But those who become savvy at their marketing say that they enjoy a more stable income and a much higher quality of projects. This chapter offers 12 marketing tactics for your consideration, along with comments and anecdotes about each from experienced freelancers.

During my first 10 years as a freelancer, I did not understand marketing. I thought marketing was an "event," but I eventually learned that marketing is a "process" after listening to other freelancers, especially fellow independents who subscribe to the STC Consulting and Independent Contracting Special Interest Group (CIC SIG) listserv.

To collect all their wisdom, I surveyed 59 members in April 2005 and asked them to share their successes with various marketing tools. I thought that if we all shared information about tools that we use, we might be able to broaden our understanding and application of tools that we might not have known about or been willing to try. Such knowledge could help us write or revise our marketing plans (see Chapter 18, *Building a Marketing Plan*).[1]

Marketing tools survey

Let's look at each tool in the order of its popularity in survey responses. As you read, please interact with the text by highlighting[2] the tools that you currently use and putting a star next to the ones you do not use (yet?). I believe this interaction with the text will be valuable to you as the Chief

---

[1] The survey is, of course, dated since many more channels for marketing have opened up, especially in social marketing. Nevertheless, it is important to recognize that in addition to social media, some older tactics are still viable and valuable.

[2] If you are reading this book in eBook form, your eReader may have a highlighting mode that you can use.

Marketing Officer of your company—you'll be able to review this chapter and consider the starred sections as possible new tactics to build a great marketing plan or refresh your current one.

Of course, the tools that you highlight will have to be appropriate for you. As one independent said, "It's important to find marketing tactics that make sense for who you are as a person. If you do not enjoy talking in front of a big group, it wouldn't make sense to set up a lot of presentations for yourself. If you perceive cold calling as being 'pushy,' cold calling might scare you." You know yourself best; select tools that will stretch you, not terrify you. But I argue that you should make your decision after you have read more about the marketing tool—so that you at least understand it before you reject it.

Business cards

The most common marketing tool, business cards, hardly needs much explanation. One survey respondent pointed out that self-printed business cards might be okay for brand new independents, but having a professionally designed and printed business card inspires confidence and exudes a comforting sense that you are a working as a permanent business, not just freelancing until a real job appears. Another independent said, "Carry your business card EVERYWHERE you go, and interject a short comment about your business whenever possible." I once landed a $10,000 contract at the gym, when someone asked me what I did for a living—I had my cards in my gym bag, and Bingo!

Networking

Independents felt it was important to ensure that all their contacts know what they do and that it was essential to ask contacts directly for advice or leads. One independent said, "I network everywhere I go, not just in professional organizations. My business is 100% based on my contacts and my personal/professional network." Another commented, "I make sure to refer to colleagues those jobs that I can't do or don't want to do, and they in turn do the same for me."

Freelancers who answered the survey defined best practices for networking, including the following:

- Attending meetings open to the public (for example, tax seminars or SCORE meetings)
- Satisfying clients so that they will refer others
- Using recommendation letters as part of their marketing portfolios
- Teaching courses at local community colleges (indirect marketing)
- Thanking people for referrals (appreciation helps!)

Several independents commented about the power of relationships:

- "The best marketing tool for my business has been developing long-term, collaborative relationships with clients. As a result, I can rely mainly on repeat business and referral to fill my project pipeline."
- "Marketing is all about building relationships. I work very hard at building a trustworthy, go-to image in all my dealings, both professional and personal."

Websites

The comments regarding websites fall into two categories: Independents' own websites (recognized mainly as a form of passive prospecting) and independents' listings on other websites. Many use their own websites in place of paper-based marketing products: "I used to give prospective clients a brochure and resume, but now I just point them to my website, and I provide printed materials only on request (mainly, samples of my work)."

Many respondents mentioned using listings in directories for freelance communicators on the websites of professional organizations (such as two that I belong to, the Boulder Writers Alliance[3] and the Professional Editors Network[4]); they also mentioned their listings on for-profit, online project matchmaking services (Elance®,[5] Guru™,[6] or STC[7]).

---

[3] http://www.bwa.org/
[4] http://pensite.org/
[5] https://www.elance.com/
[6] http://www.guru.com/
[7] http://jobs.stc.org/home/index.cfm?site_id=360

Volunteering

I have found volunteering for professional organizations to be a fail-safe marketing tactic. I work hard, produce results for the organizations that I love, and get recognized as being effective and trustworthy. This produces benefits for me: I volunteered for a local organization of human resource professionals and gained exposure for my business that brought me several nice contracts. Others volunteer for public school committees and civic groups—there are plenty of potential contacts or referrals in any group.

Print-based materials

Independents use the following printed marketing tools:

- Direct mail letters to prospective clients
- Portfolio
- Query letters
- Holiday cards

Just as with business cards, professional design and printing is essential if you want to project your best image. And if you use a mailing service, insist on stamped mail because it gets opened more than metered mail does.

Cold calls

The best survey advice about cold calls was "Be politically savvy. Learn some basic salesmanship… and be prepared, even if you're meeting an old colleague 'just' for coffee. Practice those elevator speeches and learn to articulate your own value proposition. Because I hate cold calls, I actually write entire scripts for them. This makes me more comfortable, and I sound more articulate. If I get an answering machine, I smilingly read the script. If I get a real person, I think on my feet and follow the script as much as possible."

Cold calls are not fun, but they aren't fatal. I have definitely obtained business from cold calls, and what has helped me most is to remember that I'm calling business-to-business; I'm not dialing into someone's dinner.

Offer free consultations

Many service providers in other professional fields offer a free consultation to prospective clients. For example, both my accountant and my intellectual property attorney met with me initially for an hour or more and did not charge me. This allowed both of us to size each other up—after all, we both want a long-term professional relationship. As long as the consultation time is limited, it's a good investment for everyone.

Of course, you would need to determine how this might work for your business. You may want to limit your policy, as did one respondent who said, "I offer free consultations to prospects, but not to existing clients."

Actually, I do offer free consultations to both prospective clients and my best current clients. When selling my training services, I offer free Lunch 'n Learns on my non-training days. I go to the clients' site, set up, and teach an hour of a focused topic, free of charge. My current clients love getting one hour of training for free, and employees who attend often register for my future classes in those companies, so I benefit too. Prospective clients get an opportunity to see if I can interact well with their employees and whether I am professional and effective.

When selling my medical editing services, I often am forced to offer a free hour of editing because I cannot provide samples—all of my contracts require a nondisclosure agreement. I benefit from this short editing exercise because I am able to see if their documents interest me enough to pursue this business. In some cases, I am able to offer a sample edited document because I have worked for free as a public service to a nonprofit and have cleared with them that I could share the before-and-after.

Offer free services

Offering free services as a part of your marketing plan can help you generate marketing tools that lend credibility to your campaign, and you'll also achieve enhanced visibility. Survey respondents said that they offer free services including:

- Writing articles or blog posts for publication, including professional organizations' journals or magazines: "I have offered limited free writing services to non-profits that I believed in. I could then use their name on my client list, and I felt good that I had supported organizations that I loved."

- Offering presentations at professional conferences. One participant offered: "I once won a great contract from someone in the audience after delivering a presentation at a conference."
- Writing for professional magazines such as STC's *Intercom*.[8] If possible, be sure to retain your copyright so that you can repurpose your content to your strategic advantage (as I have done with this book!)

Imprinted marketing materials

One respondent said: "I pass out bookmarks, letter openers, and such with my company name and website; people keep them and remember me years later when they need my services. I once had a client contact me for a job six years after my initial contact." I have had a similar experience; I used to give out pens imprinted with my name and website in my classes, and many years later, I was contacted by someone whose husband found my pen (it had migrated to his home office). He called me for a bid.

Newsletters

From 1995 to 2006, I mailed a quarterly newsletter to keep in touch with existing and potential clients. I sometimes received comments from readers such as this: "I always enjoy your newsletters and particularly the latest—thanks!" Bookings increased after I produced and mailed my newsletter.

I missed sending my newsletter a few quarters one year, and my gross income was lower than usual. I believe that downturn was correlated with my lack of marketing by newsletter. So, as annoying as the process of generating a newsletter is, I need to keep it up! Remember the mantra: "I don't like to produce my newsletter, but I like to have produced my newsletter."

In 2006, I switched to electronic delivery for my newsletters through Constant Contact®. Visit my newsletter archive[9] to see a few of my newsletters.

---

[8] http://www.stc.org/publications/intercom
[9] http://archive.constantcontact.com/fs037/1101250847266/archive/1102482234714.html

I receive e-mail responses from readers, and I do book business after each issue, perhaps because I am "top of mind" after I publish each edition.

Postcards

Several independents mentioned using postcards for prospecting. I have used them to advertise public offerings of my writing classes (which is, of course, an event versus a service) and for publicizing my medical editing services. I have seen effective postcards along with a lot of ineffective ones, too (poor printing quality is the worst offense).

One way to improve the quality of any postcard that you send is to engage the services of a graphic artist and a marketing copywriter.

Advertising in newspapers

I personally have not seen a lot of business flow in from direct advertising, but it is clearly a way to get one's name out there, as one independent said: "Things like advertising in local magazines and professional newsletters rarely bring in business, but they do help with name recognition, even if people can't remember why they know the name."

Just recently, I submitted a short, free advertisement to the "15-second Pitch" section of my local paper. On the day of its publication, I received a phone call from a financial planner pitching his services—good for him! I recognized a good marketer in action.

Likewise, advertising at trade shows has not been profitable for me, but one independent mentioned that "for the past two years, we've had a booth at an annual conference that caters to our target audience."

An unsurveyed category: Keeping in touch with clients

The survey did not contain any questions about tactics used to keep in touch with clients, but independents spoke up anyway:

- "If I stumble on an article related to my clients' field, I will forward it with my comments as well. This helps ensure that I stay top of mind, even when I'm not hunting down business."

- "Most of my work comes by word-of-mouth... often from someone I met or knew on a project. That person might be my main contact, or just someone who did a review at one stage or another. Cultivating a strong relationship and their trust that I am working to create excellent documentation goes a long way."
- "I use e-mail and Christmas cards for keeping in touch."

Survey conclusions

Freelancers responding to the survey offered the best marketing advice:

- "Failure to market yourself is a sure recipe for failure in business."
- "It [marketing] is the toughest part of the business."
- "The constant need to market bedevils me. I am far from mastering it."
- "You have to keep it up to ride out economic downturns. Failure to keep up the marketing means failure."
- "When you are not doing it [marketing] it seems daunting and scary; when you are doing it, it is surprising how much fun (and rewarding) it can be."

It seems clear that if you plan to survive as a business, you need to make your marketing plan reasonable and even fun. As one respondent mentioned: "Be yourself, the host or hostess of the party!"

And since you all want to succeed rather than fail, implementing incremental changes in your marketing tactics will be very effective. If you have not highlighted a tactic (or several) above that might help you, please do that now, and try to build it into your marketing plan.

CHAPTER 21

Networking for Independents

Most entrepreneurs recognize networking as the easiest, least expensive, and most productive type of marketing that they can undertake; some even boast that it is the only marketing they do. Consider networking as an opportunity to give information and referrals to others and you will be perceived as helpful and effective—resulting in future business for you. This chapter will show you how and where to make connections most effectively and provide useful tips to increase your skills. Because networking is rarely taught in business school or even in entrepreneurial training, I will suggest strategic and tactical methods to help you develop your skills.

I wrote this chapter in Anchorage, Alaska, where I was bonding with my newest grandchild. While there, I called my office and retrieved a message from the editor of one of the largest newspapers in my home city; she wanted me to train her proofreaders. Now, I didn't know this woman (let's call her Phyllis), but someone in my network (let's call her Sandy) had referred me to her. I had recently presented a pro bono seminar to a group that Sandy attended. As a result, while vacationing in Alaska, I got introduced to Phyllis through Sandy, rather than having to cold call her. My network works for me while I vacation!

Let's define networking as a perpetual series of interactions intended to cultivate mutually beneficial, nurturing relationships. Angela Nierenberg defines a good networker: "She listens, she takes in all sorts of information, and when the time is right, she will put different folks and projects together where she thinks there is a good fit" (*Nonstop Networking: How to Improve Your Life, Luck, and Career*[12, p. 73]).

Networking as intentional interaction

One fundamental difference between independents and employees is that the former view networking as an ongoing, long-range method to locate contacts and establish alliances, while the latter often consider networking to be a short-term tactic to find work when they are unemployed.

For independents, productive networking involves having a plan and working it. Earlier in this book, I have stressed the benefits of writing a business plan and, within it, a marketing plan. Your networking plan is an integral piece of your marketing plan. You can start by thinking about who, how, what, and when:

- With whom will you connect?
- How will you establish yourself as a valued resource?
- What will you do to stay in touch?
- When will you make connections?

With whom will you connect?

Independents tend to gravitate toward professional associations that attract other independents in their discipline. That's why I joined both the Society for Technical Communication (STC)[1] and the American Medical Writers Association (AMWA)[2] and attend their local and international meetings. Associations are organizations are where you can establish your specialties and demonstrate how your skills differ from those of other members. Laying this groundwork helps you convince other independents that they could and should refer business to you.

It is also absolutely necessary to attend a variety of other association and organizational meetings where you might meet potential clients. Most cities have a wealth of professional associations that you might target. Ask your clients what associations they attend; if you are a new independent, you might conduct a Web search. You can read your local newspaper's calendar section (often online) to learn more about associations in your neighborhood and ask other independents for suggestions.

For example, since one of my service lines is training people in business and technical writing, I joined PACT (Professional Association for Computer Training)[3] in Minneapolis, a local organization that attracts about 80 people a month to its breakfast meeting, most of whom are potential

---

[1] http://www.stc.org
[2] http://www.amwa.org
[3] http://pactweb.org

clients. I made it my goal to make a splash at my first meeting. I stood up and introduced myself and my business, and, when members shared their recent accomplishments, I mentioned my two recent national presentations. Fortunately, these accomplishments were also documented in PACT's printed newsletter, so I received double the publicity. Within a few months, I was invited to give a presentation to PACT and gained a few new clients.

How will you establish yourself as a valued resource?

Most articles on networking close with advice on "giving back" after you have received the benefits of networking. I prefer the more generous concept of giving without expectation, and doing so from the time you begin networking (*Nonstop Networking*[12, p. 69]).

Bob Burg,[4] a networking expert and author of *Endless Referrals*[3], says that humans are creatures of "increase"—and when we meet people who seem interested in providing increase in any area of our life, we are attracted to them.

Good networking begins by asking, "How can I help you today?"

One way to establish yourself as a giving person is to volunteer your time. For example, shortly after I joined STC, I volunteered for a committee, where I met another new member. As we worked together, we developed a mutual admiration, and she invited me to pitch my training classes to her management. This gesture resulted in about $10,000 worth of training classes in my first year in STC. Note that I was rewarded only after I had given of myself in committee work.

Another way to give to an organization is to write or speak for it. Most associations have newsletters or other formal ways to communicate with their members; I have always found these groups willing to publish useful and interesting articles with my byline and e-mail address. Often I can rework the same content for another audience, reducing production time by half.

---

[4] http://burg.com

Since all organizations have meetings, program chairs are always looking for lively, informational meeting topics. Speaking gets your name and expertise in front of potential clients in a way you could never pay for!

You say you fear public speaking? So do I, but I have learned some tricks to overcome my apprehension. I started by presenting at local STC Special Interest Group (SIG)[5] meetings, then moved on to monthly chapter meetings and, finally, to the international conference. By giving to STC, I kept improving my presentation skills until I was ready to speak at other associations. I also attend Toastmasters[6] and improv classes. Remember that no matter how confident they may appear, most professionals fear public speaking. Wise presenters take steps to overcome those fears.

In addition to increased overall visibility in the associations to which you belong, you will want to focus on your relationships with individuals. You must be able to converse fluently with everyone whom you contact. Look for someone standing alone; it is probably easier to engage one person standing alone than it is to break into a group. (For tips on how to approach a group, see Nierenberg's *Nonstop Networking*[12].)

My friend Pat O'Donnell[7] is an effective networker. She arrives at meetings earlier than most people to increase her opportunities for interaction. She doesn't stay long in one conversation; instead, she moves to a new person after five or ten minutes. Just last week she brought someone over to introduce to me—someone who could offer me a resource I needed. Then she moved on, introducing herself to a group of total strangers.

No one in the room would suspect that Pat is highly introverted; she is one of the shyest people I know. She has developed deliberate conversational skills to work around her shyness and serves as a model for anyone who would network to improve their business. Pat focuses on helping others, on providing information that could help them do their jobs better. "How can I best help you?" is her motto, and it reaps huge rewards. If you are an

---

[5] http://www.stcsig.org/cic/pages/links.htm
[6] http://www.toastmasters.org/
[7] http://odonnellpatblog.com/

introvert (and many technical communicators are), Nierenberg's chapter on networking for introverts may help.

Whatever you do in a networking situation, do not copy this unskilled networker in action:

> "Hi, I'm Mary Jones, and I develop and write employee manuals. I have produced manuals for XXX and YYY. They loved my work. Here's my business card. Whom can I contact in your organization to get some business?"

Of course, we all recognize this introduction as a poorly timed pitch/attempted close, probably fueled by desperation. I know I would have backed off immediately if Mary had approached me this way.

Let's imagine a more skillful approach:

> "Hi, I'm Mary Jones, and this is my first meeting here. Are you a member of this organization?"
>
> "Yes, I have belonged to XXX for three years. My name is George Smith, and I work for Megabucks Corporation, in the Human Resources department."
>
> "That's interesting, George. What do you do in Human Resources?" (Further questions could be "What changes have you seen in your company? In the HR field?" "How has this organization helped you?")

This conversation is all about George. Mary won't highlight her expertise until she learns enough about George and Megabucks to know if cultivating him as a contact would be good for her business. She might not even promote her business in this first contact, although she will establish what she does in a graceful way that keeps George in the limelight. She might say, "Oh, that's an interesting development. I have been involved in that issue with my client, XXXX. What did you do when that happened?" Mary thereby focuses on information-gathering, not selling.

People generally love to talk about themselves. Listening to them is a way of giving them your attention instead of demanding theirs. A good rule of thumb is to listen 80 percent of the time and talk 20 percent.

Perhaps you are thinking that you cannot imagine yourself in conversations like these. Why not arrange to role-play a networking conversation with some fellow entrepreneurs? You could even videotape or audiotape each conversation and play it back to critique your interactions. Did you listen more than you talked?

After Mary has listened to George, she will work a 30-second infomercial into the conversation. Nierenberg suggests that you create a short, engaging statement (your elevator pitch) about what you do that might prompt your listener to ask, "Really—how do you do that?"

Mary has had hardly a moment to think about her fear of talking to strangers because she has been so busy listening to George. They talk for ten minutes, after which they exchange business cards. They both move on to other conversations, but, as soon as she can, Mary writes down everything she can remember about George and Megabucks on the back of his card or in her journal. If she knows that she could help George and his company, she moves on to her next step: staying in touch.

What will you do to stay in touch?

Establishing a routine to stay in touch with your contacts requires discipline. You can maintain a paper-based contact list, but contact management software, a spreadsheet, or LinkedIn is often more useful than paper-based systems for managing the number of business cards you will collect when you are networking properly. I always write notes in my journal ("has son who played hockey for Hill Murray"; "breeds Labrador retrievers and likes to kayak") and enter them into my software along with each individual's contact information. I do this on the same day I meet potential contacts, or at least by Friday of that week.

Within a week of making a connection, I try to e-mail or call just to say I enjoyed meeting that person and to thank him or her for any information I received. Nierenberg suggests that you send a thank-you-for-talking-with-me card the same day you meet someone. When I write to new contacts, I may refer them to someone else who should get to know them. In other words, I take action to show my good intentions and to help me remember new people I meet.

Networking etiquette may not be intuitive to everyone, so I need to stress here that if George refers you to someone in his network, be sure to thank him (a handwritten card would be nice) and follow up to let him know how it worked out: Did you get the job? If so, how is it going? Also, if you are about to refer someone in your network to a client, be sure to call or e-mail the person you are referring, so the contact doesn't come as a surprise.

When will you make connections with your network?

Remember, your goal is to cultivate long-lasting relationships, not just short-term, needs-based requests for help. I try to contact those in my network personally at least twice a quarter. I see many of my contacts at meetings at least once per quarter, and I send them a newsletter consisting of 98 percent information and 2 percent marketing. I used to mail the newsletters first class every quarter with a handwritten note to each person; today, I use Constant Contact* for my newsletter.

Other ways to keep in touch include passing on information that could help a new person on your list. Mary might have learned from her meeting with George that he wants to get an advanced degree in his field, and she might forward him a link or an article about his chosen field that she comes across. As a result of this unobtrusive (giving, not asking) networking, George will probably perceive Mary as both knowledgeable and helpful.

This positive impression will assist in what is known as "top of mind" marketing. When George needs to outsource any projects, Mary's name will pop into his mind automatically. She has deliberately cultivated the actions that brand her as an effective person with helpful knowledge. You, too, can do all these things, or some of them, to improve the marketing of your business—just try a few of the steps Nierenberg suggests.

Once you are an expert at networking, teach it to others. After all, if there are only six degrees of separation between all of us, it pays to have many productive resources in your network!

A final note

As I finished this chapter after returning home from Alaska, I received an e-mail from an STC member whom I had referred to a customer of mine. She thanked me for helping her make this contact and said my customer was happy with her services—a bonus for me! At the beginning and end of my vacation, networking was working for me, even from a distance.

Operations

CHAPTER 22

Independents and the "F" Word

Many aspects of self-employment scared me at first. Marketing myself
seemed terrifying, but it paled by comparison to planning my business
finances. Since no business could possibly survive without either activity,
I had to get over my fears pretty fast. If you are fearful of all things finan-
cial, too, this chapter may help.

When I left full-time employment to start my own business, I feared the
"F" word: finance. I was vague about a lot of business principles, particularly
vague about business finances. You may have heard the saying: "What
happens in vagueness, stays in vagueness." I could not afford to continue
the way I was going.

In addition, if you believe, as I do, that the world is divided into two
groups—word people and numbers people—chances are that many, if not
most, communication independents fall into the word category and are
basically uncomfortable with numbers.

I am guilty on two counts: no real business training and no ability with
numbers. Yet I have always known—as a committed independent since
1990—that I could have understood and managed my business's finances
better. Here is the story of how I worked to transform myself from being
uncomfortable with finance to comfortable with finance.

Recognizing my "Rosie"

I was not really aware of my fear of financial matters until I took my
grandson Axel (18 months old at the time) to the Butterfly Pavilion in
Westminster, Colorado. We approached the "bug" room, and he spotted
Rosie—a five-inch live tarantula held by a cheerful volunteer. Axel ran
screaming from the room. On our next visit, he got halfway across the room
before he bolted; the visit after that, he let me hold Rosie in one hand as he
tried to tug me away from her. Then one day I found a large plastic toy
Rosie at Target and took it over to his house. He immediately picked it up

and crowed, "Gamma, I hold Rosie!" He was thrilled and insisted upon taking his plastic Rosie to show to the real Rosie.

I'm grateful to Axel for showing me how natural our fears are and how I could work through my fear of finance one step at a time. (True confession: Before I assumed my brave, tarantula-holding persona in front of Axel, I had always been terrified of spiders—but no more!) I learned that I don't need to understand my fears in order to walk through them; I just have to take action, as Axel and I did. Eleanor Roosevelt's wonderful quote about fear inspires me: "Do one thing every day that scares you."

Into action

And so, admitting my fear and loathing of all things financial, and recognizing that I had no real idea of my business's bottom line, I went to our local Small Business Development Center (SBDC)[1] and took a class in "Analyzing and Using Financial Statements," taught by Leo, a retired accountant. At first, most of the material was over my head, but I persisted and scheduled an individual appointment with Leo to apply this financial learning to my situation.[2]

Leo taught me that I need four levels of financial control for my business:

1. Record-keeping
2. Bookkeeping
3. Accounting
4. Guiding financial knowledge

I have always been compulsive about filing receipts and organizing my paper data into neatly labeled files (which is the lowest level of financial control), but I was completely ignorant about bookkeeping best practices. I had been adding categories in Quicken for years with no apparent logic— resulting in counterproductive redundancy. Nothing in my system showed my profit or loss on each of my seven service lines.

---

[1] http://www.sba.gov/content/small-business-development-centers-sbdcs
[2] If you don't have access to an SBDC, check with your local chapter of SCORE (http://-score.org.

Leo and I reworked all my categories and came up with a logical list that clearly and quickly shows me what is going on in my business.

A word here about Quicken vs. QuickBooks:

Years ago, an accountant suggested that since I was confused and frustrated by QuickBooks, it might be a good idea to use Quicken to post my expenses and income. QuickBooks, a double-entry accounting program, is more robust, but I was totally mystified by its intricacies. The only downside of Quicken is its lack of an invoicing module; however, I quickly learned to produce invoices manually. There are plenty of classes to help you learn the software.

Category list in hand, I hired Loretta as my bookkeeper to help me implement the new categories and ensure that I was posting everything correctly. She was wonderful; she did not laugh when she asked me why I had posted a certain expense in a certain place. "Why, it just seemed to make sense to me at the time!" was my weak response. Within two hours, she had totally whipped my Quicken into shape, and I felt much better as I saw my first-ever profit-and-loss statement emerge. I now have much better data to take to my accountant every January, and I understand my business better.

A new system is born

I was witnessing the emergence of a new system—a streamlined, documented way to do my record-keeping, bookkeeping, accounting, and financial planning. As I learned from Michael Gerber's *E-Myth Revisited*[7], business systems don't have to be dehumanizing. Here are three stories to prove the humanizing effects of learning to manage my numbers better.

First, my financial guru, Leo, showed up for one of our appointments with a cast on his arm. Sweet Leo is in his late seventies, and I was alarmed. He explained that he had been cleaning his gutters and had tumbled off the ladder. Sheepishly, he admitted that his wife had finally banished all ladders from the house and hired a gutter-cleaning service. Thank goodness his fall wasn't worse! What better validation that I need to hire bookkeeping and accounting help because this is outside of my core competence.

Second, hiring my bookkeeper, Loretta, opened my eyes to a better system. She is fast and smart where I'm slow and stupid. I wish I had done this years ago so I could free up the energy I need to develop my business strategy and live my passion, which is to help employees learn how to write better and edit medical documents to perfection.

And the third humanizing effect: I realize now, in a very deep place, that my students may look at words and writing and grammar rules the way I formerly looked at numbers and accounting—with great suspicion and fear. Maybe they dread writing the way I dreaded downloading my credit card information at first. Perhaps they distrust text the way I have always distrusted spreadsheets.

I feel that I now have more compassion for them and their plight because I have confronted my fear, taken action, and improved my financial understanding of my business. I thank my three leaders: Axel, Leo, and Loretta, and I look forward to conquering more of my business fears.

CHAPTER 23

The Freelancer's Biggest Worry: Losing Money Bidding Projects

Estimating and bidding jobs accurately can be fraught with emotion (especially fear). If we overbid, we might lose out to lower bidders, but if we underbid and get the contract, we lose money. There is a middle way, however; read on to learn how to bid wisely so that you will get paid fairly.

As I mentioned in Chapter 22, *Independents and the "F" Word*, I have always been vague about numbers. One result of this vagueness is a peculiar amnesia about how much time I spend on any activity, including work activities. With such a dysfunctional view of time, it is a miracle that I have survived for so long as a freelancer.

After I read Laurie Lewis's *What to Charge: Pricing Strategies for Freelancers and Consultants*[10], I now understand that my ignorance is costing me money when bidding for work on a project basis. Lewis suggests that as a general practice, we should log EVERY activity on every project and then mine those logs to understand more clearly how long the tasks of a prospective project might take. (See Chapter 24, *Time Flies! Time-tracking Software for Independents*, for a list of time-tracking and invoicing software.)

Lewis explains the whole process clearly in Chapter 3 and shows how to use logs to estimate any new project:

> For six months, keep task-oriented logs on every project you do, whether you are paid by the hour, the day, the job, or whatever. After you've used the information in your logs to price other jobs and to manage your business better, you will be convinced that the little bit of record-keeping effort was totally worthwhile (p. 34).

I'm convinced! Before I read this book, I had just estimated and bid a training customization at 3 hours—but it actually took 13 hours. Of course,

I could not charge for the 10 extra hours. You can bet that I will use this painful experience to bid more realistically next time.

Negotiating tactics

Chapter 8 of *What to Charge* shares some excellent negotiating tactics. One that I have used with success appears on page 96: "Call your suggested project rate a cap, and say you will try to make the final bill less." Another strategic suggestion is not to suggest your price right away—continue to ask questions and perhaps the client will reveal their budget for the project. In any case, you'll get more insight into the project before you commit to a price.

I was also fascinated with her triple-scenario, multiple-rate, task-based estimating method. Lewis claims "The more numbers, the better" (p. 67). She suggests that you prepare three time-estimate scenarios, and she even nicknames them:

1. Everything goes exceptionally smoothly (Cream Puff)
2. The job is fairly typical (Average)
3. Every task is more complicated than usual (Job From Hell)

By projecting different rates and possible scenarios, you provide yourself with room to negotiate based on what you understand about the project and your client's budget. You will be able to bid jobs more accurately so that you get paid a fair rate. And finally, you will avoid overbooking yourself or taking on work that you cannot complete in the allotted time frame.

I recently tracked the hours that it actually took me to deliver technical writing webinars for a client. I was astounded by the total number of hours I was spending on a variety of activities! I prepared a proposal to adjust my billing to reflect my actual costs based on my invested time. My client agreed and I now have a $10,000 annual increase in my income. What a great return on my investment of $23.95 for Lewis's book!

Who can learn from this book

Lewis's book can help three audiences: new freelancers, experienced free-lancers, and employees. New freelancers will get a glimpse into a rational method of setting rates and negotiating. Experienced freelancers will understand the value of keeping detailed task logs. (This practice had always seemed so compulsive to me, but now I am a convert.) Employees will learn how and why to keep a task log that can help them justify time estimates for projects that management may be underestimating; they will also learn some negotiating tips and tactics for their next raise or job negotiation.

Don't have time to go through the exercises suggested above? Lewis offers *Freelance Fee Setting: Quick Guide for When a Client Demands a Price NOW*[1] on Kindle ($2.99 at this writing).

---

[1] http://www.amazon.com/Freelance-Fee-Setting-Demands-ebook/dp/B0077STDEC

CHAPTER 24

Time Flies! Time-tracking Software for Independents

In the last chapter, you learned why you should track the time you spend on every task so that you can charge fairly for your services. To most effectively capture time spent, you will need a good system. Will you use your kitchen clock or a digital tool? This chapter shares 17 different time-tracking tools that you might consider.

Freelancers need to know how long our work activities take so that we can provide valid estimates of future work when asked. Knowing how long tasks take can help us prove to a client why it is impossible for us or anyone to meet unrealistic deadlines. In addition, freelancers can lose projects or lose money on projects if they cannot estimate accurately and correctly.

Laurie Lewis's book *What to Charge: Pricing Strategies for Freelancers and Consultants*[10] convinced me to track my time. However, I have never been an early adopter of technology. Instead, I typically have used my kitchen timer and scraps of paper or Excel spreadsheets to record my time. Several of my freelance friends have suggested a better way—digitally capturing time using time-tracking software.

I did my due diligence and researched some programs on the market, spending 2 hours and 27 minutes (according to my kitchen timer). I was able to narrow my options to those shown in Table 24.1, but I include the other categories so that you, too, might know what your options are if you want to track your time digitally.

Four main types of time-tracking software

Table 24.1 – Standalone—records time sheets and generates reports

Program	Website/Notes
SLIMTIMER	slimtimer.com
	Free, cloud-based
Grindstone	epiforge.com/Grindstone
	Desktop free, team option $
VeriTime Time Tracker	pcfworks.com
	Desktop shareware, Pro version $
TraxTime	spudcity.com/traxtime/
	$, free trial, Windows only
Toggl	toggl.com/
	Basic free, full-feature a$

Table 24.2 – Integrated into accounting systems

Program	Website/Notes
Quickbooks	quickbooks.intuit.com/
	$; desktop Mac and Windows; payroll
SpringAhead	springahead.com/
	$, free demo; payroll
Freshbooks	freshbooks.com/
	$, free trial; cloud, mobile; invoicing and accounting

Table 24.3 – Integrated into billing system—used to generate invoices, especially used by contractors and professionals such as lawyers

Program	Website/Notes
Easy Projects	easyprojects.net
	$, 15-day free trial, $ to purchase based on # of users; cloud; invoicing, reports
Klok	getklok.com
	$, free trial; cloud, desktop
Intervals	myintervals.com
	$, free trial, cloud, $ to purchase based on # of users, invoicing
Bill4Time	bill4time.com
	$, free trial, cloud, mobile app
Harvest	getharvest.com
	$ subscription, free trial; cloud, Mac app; add contractors
OfficeTime	officetime.net
	$, free trial; Mac, PC, iPhone, iPad, desktop
HourGuard Timesheet Software	nchsoftware.com/
	$, free trial; Mac, PC; several components can be bundled

Table 24.4 – Integrated into project management systems

Program	Website/Notes
Dovico Timesheet	dovico.com/
	free for one subscription, $ for more, free trial; cloud, mobile app
Paymo	paymo.biz
	free for one user, $ for more; desktop, mobile, cloud; online invoices

You will find an interesting matrix of time-tracking software on Wikipedia (Comparison of time tracking software).[18] It reviews many other programs not listed here. Whatever you choose, perform your normal due diligence—there is a learning curve to any software product, so you won't want to be changing products frequently.

---

[18] http://en.wikipedia.org/wiki/Comparison_of_time_tracking_software

CHAPTER 25

Time Matters

Since the only thing that most freelance independents can sell is time and time is a limited resource, it is essential that we organize our own time efficiently to maximize our billable hours. This chapter offers some tips to organize your time.

There I was, tooling over Berthoud Pass in a whiteout, only half an hour away from the cross-country ski trails near Winter Park, Colorado. I was probably driving way too fast for conditions, leading the pack behind me, emboldened by brand-new snow tires and 35 years' experience driving on snow and ice in Alaska and Minnesota.

Suddenly, I saw an oil truck looming ahead. Gradually, I slowed to its crawling pace (10 mph), and watched the queue build behind me. And that's how we proceeded down from the pass: single file at a snail's pace. When we finally dumped out onto the highway, there were 40 or more cars behind me.

Immediately, I thought about the book in my briefcase, *Getting Things Done: The Art of Stress-Free Productivity*[1] by David Allen.[1] Allen argues that we fail to do a better job of organizing ourselves because we get stuck behind (or under) psychological blocks. Our only strategic hope for accomplishing more is to clear these blocks and proceed tactically.

Ha! Easier said than done. I was not able to clear that oil truck ahead of me, but, of course, slowing down was probably a good idea, given the conditions. That's an external blockage. But how can we reduce the mental blocks that we create in our minds?

After a morning of skiing, I read Allen's book and became more productive by adopting many of his tactics (but not all; more about that later). I wanted to achieve Allen's stress-free promise. Allen defines stress-free as having a "mind like water." He explains: "Imagine throwing a pebble into a still

---

[1] http://www.davidco.com/

pond. How does the water respond?…[T]otally appropriately to the force and mass of the input; then it returns to calm. It doesn't overreact or under-react" (pp. 10–11).

Allen suggests not carrying too much around in your head. Instead, collect your tasks, then assess whether you want to commit to any or all of them. If you do decide to commit or involve yourself, then create a system to outline and track your actions.

Step 1: Collect

I learned from Allen to collect every "pebble" or action in one location as tasks flow in from my e-mail, daily journal, mailbox, phone messages, text messages, and mental memory. This collection habit seems to take a lot of time, and it is overwhelming at first. Allen recommends several days for your first collection. And if you have been out of the office or buried in a project, your collection will take another big chunk of time (although not as big as the first time).

I recently returned from a ten-day training trip and felt totally overwhelmed collecting the tasks that had piled up. I was blocked again and could not bear to be in my office. I left to wash my poor snow-begrimed car and when I returned, I was somehow able to tackle the collection again. Another block washed away!

Step 2: Commit or pass

Once the tasks are in one place, I sit with the collection bucket and sift through it, top item first. It is very important to take each item and dispose of it in order…no fair shuffling it to the bottom of the pile. This is hard.

I base my decisions on three criteria: context, time, and energy required. I complete any worthy tasks that need less than two minutes (oh, that feels good). Tasks that need longer time commitments are probably new projects or parts of existing ones. If a task signals a new project, I make a new project file. In the front of the file, I sketch a flow chart for the project (eventually to become a digital flow chart). I log the project onto a master project list.

Then I log the task into my Outlook task file, with an appropriate scheduled date and category.

Of course, I can pass on any task rather than commit to it. I am in charge of my schedule, after all.

Step 3: Review and track

My active project files are twelve inches from my desk in one attractive notebook, and the master list sits on my desk. I can review the entire list in a glance, perhaps while waiting for a conference call to begin. I print my task list daily, highlight critical upcoming tasks, and remove completed ones (or cross out items that I decide not to do at all because they are not useful, as Allen suggests). Then I make a list for the day and get to work. Allen doesn't agree with making daily lists, but it's a habit I can't seem to break. Crossing out completed tasks just seems so satisfying!

Another benefit of this system is that it leads to better physical organization. The book is not really about decluttering—but that happens. It isn't about organizing files better—but that happens, too. I even reorganized my recipes without actually planning to do so—call me the Accidental Organizer.

I can't believe how much more productive I feel using this system; I even sleep better. Instead of a huge physical in-box to sift through every day (Where is that bid?), I have two lists to review and a set of very organized files to pull the bid out of.

Of course, new things show up ad hoc, but they don't create my schedule: I create my schedule. New things go into the collection (step 1) and the rest quickly becomes automatic. Allen says this process is psychological: "The minute that a list is not totally current, your brain will not trust the system" (p. 181). That means you aren't able to devote your full psychic attention to the work at hand. He claims this system "enables the brain to move toward more elegant and productive activity" (p. 181), something that happens only when you know everything that you are not doing, but could be doing if you decided to (you are in charge of your schedule, not others).

I make my conversion sound so simple. In fact, I accepted this new program just as I accept all new ideas: I have to be dragged kicking and screaming toward change. I first said no. The ideas in the book seemed either too complex or too simple. That's OK; change is strange. I kept coming back to the book, though, and soon adopted many of Allen's ideas. Again, his tactical suggestions help. For example, "One of the best ways to increase your energy is to close some of your loops [runway, or current actions]. So always be sure to have some easy loops to close, right at hand" (p. 95).

I find that accomplishing simple tasks such as calling for my dental appointment can provide momentum to my day—"Yes, I am moving ahead"—and allow me to proceed with confidence to bigger, more strategic tasks.

Soon, I was defining the edges of my work and managing huge numbers of open loops. This positive experience with time has made me realize that time is finite. I can't make more time for myself, but my energy level—that can be adjusted upward. If I can keep my work energy high by not being blocked, I can use my time most wisely to earn more money.

Allen helped me discover that I do have all the time I need to do all the things I truly need to do. When my mind is like water, I have no blocks to keep me from producing powerfully. When I am blocked, my brain is moving at 10 mph, just like all those cars crawling down Berthoud Pass.

CHAPTER 26
A Room with a Window

The last three chapters have focused on time tracking and time management, and appropriately so: Freelancers can only sell time, so having more time to sell probably means greater profits. But having time available can be dependent on how well you are organized in your workplace. This chapter shares some suggestions for creating good work space that have been shared by fellow freelancers (members of the Society for Technical Communication's (STC) Consulting and Independent Contracting Special Interest Group[1]). You will learn how others have managed to organize themselves and save their time.

I was lucky in my last two jobs before I went independent. In both companies, I had an office with a window and a door—and messy stacks of papers. When I went freelance in 1990, I moved to my home office in the basement. I had a door but not much of a window. Gradually, I have upgraded my office space through several houses; my current office has four windows, soothing green walls, and a functional configuration of furniture.

However, the mess continues. I know very well that my physical disorganization equals time lost; that is the theme of this chapter: You have to spend time organizing yourself so that you can save time in your operations.

Why be organized?

The consensus among my fellow independents is that being organized saves you time, makes you look more professional, and allows you to get more done. Monique Semp of Write Quick Inc.[2] claims, "Being organized is essential. You don't want to waste time looking for things that you know are 'somewhere.' This applies to paperwork, e-mail, hard drive folders, and browser bookmarks. And for most people, being organized lowers our day-to-day stress level."

---

[1] http://www.stcsig.org/cic/index.html
[2] http://writequickinc.com/

Yes, spending valuable time looking for my "lost" cell phone truly stressed me recently. (Note to self: Always put the cell phone back in your purse before exiting the car; otherwise, it may get knocked under the car seat and hide for hours.)

Here are other possible disasters that may happen when you aren't organized, offered by fellow freelancer Janet S. Clifford:

- Losing a client's contact information or not returning a call promptly may result in lost business.
- Missing deadlines or arriving late to client meetings may result in losing face and losing that client's valuable business.
- Losing or destroying files could result in legal or financial problems.

Organizing your office to save time

Start to recognize the dysfunction in your office organization. I see now that I slide into disorganization long before I recognize the problem. In fact, I think my business has only been well organized once—when I moved from Minnesota to Colorado in 2005. Because my new office was one half the size of my old one, I had to downsize all my furniture and also purge 15 years' worth of paper files. However, once on the ground in Colorado, I just plunked my lean files in cabinets and hit the street to market myself. My office quickly became disorganized again.

It wasn't until I read all the survey comments about finding files easily that I realized how seriously dysfunctional my filing system was. I often could not find any files until it was actually too late to use them.

Once I recognized my problem, I followed a project management strategy that has worked well for me. I divided every task into the smallest chunks possible. For example, I set a realistic small chunk of time every day to de-clutter "the impossible stack of paper" (maybe 10 minutes a day? First or last thing every day?). I have Outlook remind me every day to perform this task. I know that if I tried to commit a full day to these tasks, I would run screaming from the room. But 10 or 15 minutes a day, if done compulsively, can work wonders. Need to miss a day? Double up the next day. The net result of working a chunked schedule (a little bit every day) will be "mission accomplished."

You might consider hiring a consultant to help get yourself on the right path; I have hired consultants to audit my office organization and feng shui and have always been pleased with the results. Recently, I decided to "think like an organizing consultant" and figure a better way to organize my projects. I implemented a new, low-tech tool for consolidating about 20 ongoing projects that had been previously scattered all over my office.

I found a nice, large notebook imprinted with photos (so I enjoy handling it). Inside, I put plastic pockets into which I can slip relevant papers, each labeled for a separate project and alphabetized. The first page in each sleeve is a flowchart of tasks I need to do for each project. After I finished a brutal, week-long client project, for example, I flipped through each project sleeve, noting tasks that I could now turn my attention to. Having everything in one place (a notebook that I can carry around if I have to) has reduced the nagging stress that can result from juggling multiple projects and trying to find the related paperwork. Of course, I could use paper files to store all this information, but the notebook has the advantage of being portable and inviting.

Another freelancer suggested a way to deal with paper that you might or might not need in the future: "Create a chronological file and put in it everything that is not client specific or financial or that otherwise has a regular folder (like auto repairs or your will). You will save oodles of time filing and trying to decide whether to file or toss. You toss when the chronological file is full, pulling from the back where the materials are now six months to one year old; it is very easy to know whether you still need the item or can toss it."

Consider using downtime or slow times between projects, perhaps over holidays, to organize your office, and always recognize that you would have to do this kind of organization if you were employed, but then, of course, you would be paid for it instead of using up your valuable billable time.

Consider subscribing to David Allen's free, educational newsletter[3] as one step toward improving your own productivity. You might also review his tips in Chapter 25, *Time Matters*.

It is clear that we must organize ourselves so that we can reap the benefits of our independent businesses. We can have the best business plan or marketing plan on the planet, but if our operations aren't running smoothly and productively, we will simply not be productive. I have found that when I feel more organized, I feel less stressed. It's all good.

---

[3] http://www.davidco.com/individuals/productive-living-newsletter

Bibliography

Available online at: textdoctor.com/business-matters-bibliography.

[1] Allen, David. *Getting Things Done: The Art of Stress-Free Productivity.* Penguin Group. New York. 2001.

[2] Angier, Bradford. *Looking for Gold: The Modern Prospector's Handbook.* Stackpole Books. Harrisburg, PA. 1980.

[3] Burg, Bob. *Endless Referrals: Network Your Everyday Contacts into Sales.* Mc-Graw-Hill, Contemporary Books. New York. 3rd ed. 2005.

[4] Cain, Susan. *Quiet: The Power of Introverts in a World That Can't Stop Talking.* Random House. New York. 2013.

[5] "Womenomics: Feminist Management Theorists Are Flirting With Some Dangerous Arguments." *The Economist.* (December 30, 2009). Online at: http://www.economist.com/node/15172746, accessed Oct. 11, 2013.

[6] "Fitter with friends." *The Economist.* (September 19, 2009). Online at: http://www.economist.com/node/14446710, accessed Oct. 11, 2013.

[7] Gerber, Michael. *The E-Myth Revisited.* Harper Collins. New York. 2001.

[8] Hall, Stacey and Jan Brogniez. *Attracting Perfect Customers: The Power of Strategic Synchronicity.* Berret Koehler. San Francisco. 2001.

[9] Levinson, Jay Conrad. *Guerilla Marketing.* Houghton Mifflin Company. 3rd ed. Boston. 1998.

[10] Lewis, Laurie. *What to Charge: Pricing Strategies for Freelancers and Consultants.* Outskirts Press, Inc. 2nd ed. Denver, Colorado. 2012.

[11] Littlepage, Dean (Guest Curator). *Gold Fever in the North: The Alaska-Yukon Gold Rush Era.* Anchorage Museum of History and Art. Anchorage, Alaska. 1997.

[12] Nierenberg, Angela. *Nonstop Networking: How to Improve Your Life, Luck, and Career.* Capital Books. Herndon, VA. 2002.

[13] Rath, Tom. *StrengthsFinder 2.0.* Gallup Press. New York. 2007.

Index

Colophon

About the Author

Dr. Elizabeth (Bette) Frick of the Text Doctor LLC[2] teaches writing and communication to employees of corporations and governments in the Denver Metro area, nationally, and internationally. Bette holds a PhD in English from the University of Minnesota and served as president of the Twin Cities chapter of STC from 2003–2004. She is a Fellow of the Society for Technical Communication (STC) and serves on the *Intercom* Editorial Advisory Panel.

Dr. Frick is also board-certified as a medical editor by the Board of Editors in the Life Sciences (BELS)[3] and serves as the Immediate Past President of the American Medical Writers Association Rocky Mountain Chapter (AMWA-RMC).[4] She recently completed requirements for the highest Toastmasters[5] award, the Distinguished Toastmaster (DTM).

About XML Press

XML Press (http://xmlpress.net) was founded in 2008 to publish content that helps technical communicators be more effective. Our publications support managers, social media practitioners, technical communicators, and content strategists and the engineers who support their efforts.

Our publications are available through most retailers, and discounted pricing is available for volume purchases for business, educational, or promotional use. For more information, send email to orders@xmlpress.net or call us at (970) 231-3624.

---

[2] http://www.textdoctor.com
[3] http://bels.org/
[4] http://www.amwa-rmc.org/
[5] http://www.toastmasters.org